The Coming Buddha
ARIYA METTEYYA

Sayagyi U Chit Tin

Assisted by
William Pruitt, PhD.

BUDDHIST PUBLICATION SOCIETY
KANDY SRI LANKA

Published in 1992

Buddhist Publication Society
P.O. Box 61
54, Sangharaja Mawatha
Kandy, Sri Lanka

2nd revised edition

ISBN 955-24-0098-8

Originally published in 1988 as Dhammadāna Series 7 by the Sayagyi U Ba Khin Memorial Trust, U.K. This 2nd revised edition is published in the Wheel Series with the consent of the author and the original publisher.

The cover photograph of a bronze image of the Bodhisatta Metteyya is from G.H. Luce's *Old Burma-Early Pagán* (3 vols., 1969-1970), used with the kind permission of the publisher J.J. Augustin.

Printed in Sri Lanka by
Karunaratne & Sons Ltd.
Colombo 10

THE WHEEL PUBLICATION NO. 381/383

Contents

Dedicated to our much revered teacher
the late ***Sayagyi U Ba Khin*** *(Thray Sitthu)*

List of Abbreviations

Unless otherwise stated, all editions are by the Pali Text Society.

A = Aṅguttara Nikāya (trans., GS).

Anāg = Anāgatavaṃsa, editions used: JPTS, 1886, pp. 33-53 (Minayeff, ed.), and Ernst Leumann, *Maitreya-samiti, das Zukunftsideal der Buddhisten* (Strassburg: Karl J. Trubner, 1919; Pāḷi text, pp. 184-191; notes, pp. 192-226).

As = Atthasālinī (trans., Expos.).

BN 630/862 = Bibliotheque nationale, Pali mss. 630 and 862, commentary on Anāg. We thank Mme J. Filliozat for making available a copy of her transcription of this text.

BT = *Buddhism in Translation* (trans. by H.C. Warren).

Bv-a = Buddhavaṃsa-aṭṭhakathā (Madhuravilāsinī) (trans., CSM).

CB = *Chronicle of Buddhas* (Buddhavaṃsa).

CPD = A Critical Pāli Dictionary (Copenhagen, 1924 —).

CSM = *The Clarifier of the Sweet Meaning* (trans. of Bv-a).

Culte = Mohan Wijayaratna, *Le Culte des dieux chez les bouddhistes singhalais* (Paris: Cerf, 1987).

D = Dīgha-nikāya (trans., DB, THIH, TS).

DB = *Dialogues of the Buddha* (D).

Dbk = Dasabodhisattuppattikathā *(The Birth-stories of the Ten Bodhisattas)* (the first number refers to the trans., the second number to the Pāḷi text).

Dbu = Dasabodhisatta-uddesa (ed. and French trans. by F. Martini [BEFEO 36, 2 (1936), pp. 287-390]. The first number refers to the French trans., the second number to the Pāḷi text).

DPPN = Dictionary of Pāli Proper Names.

D-ṭ = Dīgha-nikāya-ṭīkā.

Dvp = Dasavatthuppakaraṇa (ed. and trans. by J. Ver Eecke, EFEO [1976]. The first number refers to the Pāḷi text, the second number to the French trans.).

Expos. = *The Expositor* (As).
GD = *The Group of Discourses* (Sn).
GS = *The Gradual Sayings* (A).
Illus. =*The Illustrator of Ultimate Meaning* (Paramatthajotikā I).
Ja = Jātaka.
JPTS = *The Journal of the Pali Text Society*.
KS = *The Kindred Sayings* (S).
M = Majjhima-nikāya (trans., MLS).
MB = *The Manuals of Buddhism* by Ledi Sayadaw (Union of Buddha Sāsana Council, 1965).
MLS = *The Middle Length Sayings* (M).
Moh = Mohavicchedanī.
Mp = Manorathapūraṇī (commentary on A).
PED = *The Pali-English Dictionary*.
Pj II = Paramatthajotikā (commentary on Sn).
Sīh = Sīhaḷavatthuppakaraṇa (ed. and trans. by J. Ver Eecke, EFEO [1980]).
Sn = Suttanipāta (trans., GD).
Sp = Samantapāsādikā (commentary on the Vinaya Piṭaka).
Spk = Sāratthappakāsinī (commentary on the Saṃyutta-nikāya).
Sv = Sumaṅgalavilāsinī (commentary on D).
Th = Theragāthā.
Th-a = Theragāthā-aṭṭhakathā (Paramatthadīpanī V).
Treatise = "A Treatise on the Pāramīs," *The All-Embracing Net of Views* (Buddhist Publication Society 1978).
THIH = *Thus Have I Heard* (trans. of D by Maurice Walshe, London: Wisdom Publications, 1987).
TS = *Ten Suttas from Dīgha Nikāya* (Rangoon: Burma Piṭaka Association, 1984).
v(v) = verse(s)
Vism = Visuddhimagga.

Namo Tassa Bhagavato Arahato Sammāsambuddhassa

INTRODUCTION

We have gathered here all the information we could find in the Theravāda tradition concerning the coming Buddha.[1] In Myanmar (Burma) and Sri Lanka, the coming Buddha is generally spoken of as Ariya Metteyya, the Noble Metteyya.[2] The term Ariya was already added to the name in some post-canonical Pāḷi texts, and it shows the deep respect felt for the Bodhisatta who will attain Awakening in the best of conditions. Indeed, all aspects of his career as a Buddha rank among the highest achievements of Buddhas of the past as recorded in the Buddhavaṃsa *(The Chronicle of Buddhas).*

It is only natural that over the years many people have aspired to meet Buddha Ariya Metteyya—not only because it has become less common for people to attain Awakening, but also because of a natural desire to encounter such a rare occasion. In his introduction to his edition and translation of the Dasabodhisattuppattikathā *(The Birth Stories of the Ten Bodhisattas)*, Ven. H. Saddhatissa has cited several texts included in

---

[1]One text, the Mahāsampiṇḍanidāna, was not available to us. For the story in it concerning Ven. Mahā-Kassapa, see Dbk, pp. 43-45. According to this text, the body of an Arahat named Kassapa who lived after the time of the Buddha is inside Kukkuṭasampāta Mountain and will come out at the time of the next Buddha to be cremated then.

Some works which include discussions of the material found in Pāḷi texts have not added any new information, and so are not quoted. See, for example, Emile Abegg, *Der Messiasglaube in Indian und Iran* (Berlin: Walter de Gruyter, 1928); Emil Abegg, "Der Buddha Maitreya," *Mitteilunger der Schwizerischen Gestellschaft der Freunde Ostasiasticher Kultur*, VII (1945), pp. 7-37. For a discussion of the importance of Metteyya in Sri Lanka, see *Culte*, pp. 86-96.

[2]The name is also shortened in Myanmar to Arimetteyya.

Pāḷi commentaries and chronicles and in Sinhalese Buddhist texts in which the writers express the wish to meet the coming Buddha.[1]

The commentary on the Jātaka stories ends with a poem in which the writer aspires to be with the Bodhisatta Metteyya in the Tusita Deva world and to receive a sure prediction of future Buddhahood from him when he becomes a Buddha.[2] Sinhalese versions of the Visuddhimagga end with a poem in which the writer aspires to rebirth in the Tāvatiṃsa Deva world and then to final liberation under Buddha Metteyya.[3] Ven. Saddhatissa attributes these verses to Ācariya Buddhaghosa, but they seem to be written by a copyist. Another aspiration to encounter Buddha Metteyya is found at the end of Sinhalese manuscripts of Ācariya Buddhaghosa's Atthasālinī.[4]

Ven. Saddhatissa also cites many instances from the Pāḷi chronicles (Mahāvaṃsa and Cūlavaṃsa) in which Sinhalese kings honoured Metteyya.[5] King Duṭṭhagāmaṇī of the second century B.C. was considered to be destined to become the next Buddha's chief disciple.

Royalty and high-ranking officials in Myanmar often made similar aspirations. This seems to have led to building pagodas with five sides at Pagan. Paul Strachan points out that with the Dhamma-Yazika Pagoda [Dhamma-Rājika Pagoda], completed in 1196 by King Sithu II, "The addition of a fifth side to temple and stupa ground plans in Myanmar is without precedent throughout the Buddhist world and the Burmese were possibly the first society throughout the world to attempt this pentagonal type of plan for a major architectural work. The origins of this

---

[1]See pp. 32-43.

[2]These verses are given in Pāḷi and English in Dbk, pp. 381. They are not included in the English translation of the Jātaka.

[3]*The Path of Purification*, pp. 837f. and Dbk, p. 40.

[4]*Expos.*, p. 542.

[5]See Dbk, pp. 42f.

movement lie in contemporary religious thought: the cults of Metteyya, the future buddha [sic], and the present cycle of five buddhas."[1] Two thirteenth-century inscriptions at the temple in Buddha Gayā record that repairs on the temple were carried out through the generosity of King Kyawswa of Myanmar, and the concluding verse is an aspiration to become a disciple of Buddha Metteyya.[2] As in Sri Lanka, many Buddhist texts end with the aspiration to meet Buddha Ariya Metteyya.

Just as the future Buddha Metteyya became more important for Buddhists as the centuries went by, many of the texts giving information about him are fairly late. The Anāgatavaṃsa is said to have been written by the author of the Mohavicchedanī, Ācariya Kassapa (1160-1230 A.D.).[3] It is very difficult to know how far back information goes when it is given in the Pāḷi commentaries, sub-commentaries, chronicles, and other texts written down after the canon. We have given all the information available to us that is part of the Theravāda tradition, but we must be careful to remember that texts such as the Dasabodhisattuppattikathā *(The Birth Stories of the Ten Bodhisattas)*, the Dasabodhisatta-uddesa, the Dasavatthuppakaraṇa, and the Sīhaḷavatthupakaraṇa are late works containing information that was likely added at a relatively late date. This is especially evident in the many variants in various texts for names and numbers.

It takes more than just a wish if a person is to encounter a Buddha and attain Nibbāna. Sayagyi U Ba Khin taught his meditation students that they must practise *sīla, samādhi,* and *paññā* (virtue, concentration, and wisdom) as Buddha Gotama taught we should. Sayagyi U Ba Khin made every effort to

---

[1] *Pagan, Art and Architecture of Old Burma* (Whiting Bay: Kiscadale Publications, 1989), p. 122. See also p. 32.

[2] See Dipak K. Barua, *Buddha Gaya Temple: Its History* (Buddha Gaya Temple Management Committee, 1981), pp. 195-200.

[3] According to the Gandhavaṃsa (61, 1). See K.R. Norman, *Pali Literature* (Wiesbaden: Otto Harrassowitz, 1983), pp. 147, 161.

ensure that his own practice and teachings were consistent with what his teachers passed on to him and with the Teachings of the Buddha in the Pāḷi Canon and commentaries.

There are many pressures in the world today to modify the Teachings of the Buddha. The Buddha foresaw that this would happen and warned his disciples to be careful to maintain the practice just as he had taught them. Ven. Mahā-Kassapa convened the First Buddhist Council shortly after the Buddha's demise in order to rehearse the Teachings. The Saṅgha has kept these Teachings intact over the centuries, and the Sixth Buddhist Council, held in Myanmar in 1954-1956, was the most recent effort to ensure that the Tipiṭaka, the three collections of texts, is kept pure.

Sayagyi U Ba Khin repeated the Burmese tradition that those who live in accordance with these Teachings will meet Buddha Ariya Metteyya. It is even believed that the coming Buddha's power will be such that he will be able to reach people who have lived up to the Teachings in this life but who have done deeds in the past which lead to their being born in lower realms before he comes. Some hints of this are found in Pāḷi texts which show the power of sharing merits.

Sayagyi also often repeated a saying of the Buddha's found in Dhammapada verse 354: *sabbadānaṃ dhammadānaṃ jināti.* "The gift of the Dhamma surpasses all other gifts." This, of course, does not mean that we should not give material gifts. Sayagyi himself was always very generous with gifts to the Saṅgha and others. But the gift of the Dhamma can only be given while the Teachings of a Buddha are available, and by laying emphasis on this quotation of the Buddha's, Sayagyi reminded us that we must never become so involved in material considerations that we neglect the most important gift of all. (See also page 21 below. If we assume that Bodhisatta Metteyya's last human life before attaining Buddhahood is during a Buddha's Dispensation, he would be able to give the gift of the Dhamma, unlike Vessantara, who lived outside such a period.)

May all make the right effort here and now in this life so that they will attain Nibbāna!

Introduction to the Revised Edition

This new edition includes corrections and additions to the first two editions. We wish to thank Venerable Bhikkhu Bodhi and Mr A.G.S. Kariyawasam of the Buddhist Publication Society for their suggestions for this second revision of our text, including several revisions in the translation of the Anāgatavaṃsa. For reasons of space, we have not included the Pāḷi text of the Anāgatavaṃsa. Mother Sayamagyi and I were pleased that the first revised edition of this text was included among the publications marking the tenth anniversary of our coming out of Myanmar to continue our work in teaching the Buddha-Dhamma in the tradition of our esteemed teacher Sayagyi U Ba Khin. We hope that this new edition in the *Wheel* series will make the text available to a larger audience.

Sayagyi U Chit Tin
International Meditation Centre
Heddington, Calne, U.K.
October 12, 1991

THE BODHISATTA METTEYYA

Uttamo Metteyyo Rāmo Pasenadi Kosalo ca
Abhibhū Dīghasoni ca Caṇḍani ca Subho
Todeyyabrāhmaṇo
Nālāgiri Palaleyyo bodhisattā anukkamena
Saṃbodhiṃ labhanti anāgate.

(Buddha Gotama predicted as follows:)

In the future (ten) Bodhisattas will attain full awakening in the following order: the most honourable (Ariya) Metteyya, (King) Rāma, (King) Pasenadi of Kosala, (the Deva) Abhibhu, (the Asura Deva) Dīghasoni, (the Brahman) Caṇḍani, (the young man) Subha, the Brahman Todeyya, (the elephant) Nālāgiri, and (the elephant) Palaleyya.[1]

The most important aspiration for any individual is to aim for the true liberation of attaining Nibbāna. When a person is able

---

[1]These verses begin the printed Burmese texts consulted: Dipeyin Sayadaw, *Anāgatavaṃsa* (Yangon: Icchāsaya Piṭaka Printing Press); Maung Ba Pe, *Anāgatavaṅ kyam*: (Yangon: Tuiṅ:ok Bhā:mā:, 1907); and the anonymous *Anāgatavaṅ kyam:* (Yangon: Kawimyakmhan, 1924). In this translation, we include in brackets the information the authors supply in their word-by-word translation of the Pāḷi into Burmese. The wording is very close to that found in a Burmese manuscript quoted by Minayeff (JPTS, 1883, p. 37), in Dbu, (p. 334), and in a Burmese *nissaya* (word-by-word translation), dated 1842, of the Anāgatavaṃsa in the Museum fur Indische Kunst, Berlin (Hs-Birm 3) (see No. 88 [p. 117] in Heinz Bechert, Daw Khin Khin Su, Daw Tin Tin Myint, *Burmese Manuscripts, part 1, Verzeichnis der Orientalischen Handschriften in Deutschland*, Band XXIII, 1 (Wiesbaden: Franz Steiner, 1979). Dbu has the following variants for names: Dīghajaṅghi for Dīghasoni and Soṇa for Caṇḍani; the lines quoted by Minayeff (and cited in Dbk, p. 17) give Saṃkacca for Caṇḍani; Hs-Birm 3 has Saṃcicca for Caṇḍani, all three texts have Pālileyyo for Palaleyyo.

to make this resolve in the presence of a Teaching Buddha and get a sure prediction from him, he or she becomes one who is intent on Awakening, a Bodhisatta.[1] There are three types of Bodhisattas:

(1) those who aspire to become Awakened as a disciple of a Teaching Buddha:
 (a) ordinary disciples *(pakati-sāvaka)*,
 (b) eighty leading disciples *(mahā-sāvaka)*, and
 (c) two chief disciples *(agga-sāvaka)*;
(2) those who aspire to become Awakened through their own efforts but who will not teach others the way to Awakening *(pacceka-bodhisatta)*, and
(3) those who aspire to become Awakened through their own efforts and who will teach others the way to Awakening *(mahā-bodhisatta)*.[2]

In this paper, we will concentrate on the last type of Bodhisatta, with particular reference to the next Buddha, Metteyya.[3]

It is natural that interest in the coming Buddha has grown as the years go by. When Buddha Gotama was alive, most of the people's efforts went to practising his Teachings and attaining Awakening. Immediately after his demise, his Teachings were collected, and, since that time, great care has gone into maintaining their purity in order that they may remain effective.

The number of those who attain Nibbāna has decreased as time goes by, and so people are inclined instead to think of meeting the next Buddha and achieving Awakening under him.[4] It is important that the practice of the Buddha's Teachings not be neglected, however. It is not wishful thinking that enables us

---

[1]Only a Teaching Buddha has the ability to see if the aspiration will be fulfilled. See *Treatise*, p. 263 under "(4) The Sight of the Master."

[2]See *Treatise*, p. 303. These are also mentioned in the introduction to Th-a.

[3]His name is also given as Ariya Metteyya.

[4]See Ven. H. Saddhatissa's introduction to Dbk, p. 33.

to encounter a Buddha, but developing the ten perfections and advancing as far as possible in the practice of a Buddha's Teachings when available. This is particularly important today as the Buddha's Teachings are on the decline and it becomes easier and easier to fall into the four lower planes of existence. If this should happen, it is very unlikely that a person would meet the next Buddha.

A Teaching Buddha is the greatest of all beings, and the preparation for achieving this state of a Supreme Awakened One *(sammāsambuddha)* takes longer than the preparation to attain Awakening as a disciple or a Pacceka Buddha.

In the commentaries on the Pāḷi Canon, the preparation of a Mahā-bodhisatta is explained in detail. This Great Being *(mahāsatta)* will develop the ten perfections *(pāramī)* longer and to a higher degree than the lesser types of Bodhisattas. A person who becomes Awakened as an ordinary disciple of a Teaching Buddha must work on the ten perfections for ten to one hundred thousand aeons.[1] Leading disciples must prepare one hundred thousand aeons. Chief disciples work for one incalculable and one hundred thousand aeons. To become a Pacceka Buddha requires two incalculable aeons. But a man working to become a Teaching Buddha develops the perfections on three levels, making thirty perfections in all.[2] The three levels of perfections mean the sacrifice of external possessions for the ordinary level, the sacrifice of any of one's limbs for the middle level, and the sacrifice of one's life for the highest level.[3]

---

[1]See Sayagyi U Ba Khin, *Dhamma Texts*, pp. 53f.; CSM, p. 88; and *The Path of Purification* (Vism), XIII 16. In CSM, the ordinary disciple is not mentioned and the time given for the Pacceka Buddha is two incalculables and one hundred thousand aeons. The figures we have given are based on how far back the various Bodhisattas can recollect as given in Vism.

[2]See *Treatise*, pp. 312-314; CSM, pp. 23, 89, 162. They are also mentioned at Dh-a I 84 and Ja I 25. The Jātaka stories illustrating the highest perfections in the case of Buddha Gotama are given in CSM (pp. 89-92).

[3]See CSM, pp. 89, 162, and *Treatise*, p. 313.

Several other interpretations for the three levels are given,[1] and some of these are of interest for meditators today. The three levels can be understood to mean: (1) rejoicing in other people's merits, (2) encouraging other people to practise the Teachings, (3) practising oneself. Or, they can be taken to mean that acquiring merit and knowledge on the first level leads to life in happy states, on the second level it leads to attaining Nibbāna oneself, and on the third level it leads to aiding others to attain both these types of happiness.

The Great Bodhisatta achieves the three levels of the perfection of giving *(dāna)* by giving (1) his belongings, children, and wife; (2) his limbs; and (3) his life. He will not transgress virtue *(sīla)* on account of these three. He fulfils renunciation *(nekkhamma)* by giving up these three after cutting off all attachment to them. By rooting out all craving for these three, he is able to discriminate between what is beneficial or harmful to beings—thus perfecting wisdom *(paññā)*. The three levels of energy *(viriya)* are reached by striving to relinquish these three. Through patience *(khanti)* he endures obstacles to his belongings, limbs, and life. He will not abandon truthfulness *(sacca)* on account of these three. His resolution *(adhiṭṭhāna)* is unshakeable even if these three are destroyed. He maintains loving kindness *(mettā)* towards others even though they destroy these three. He perfects equanimity *(upekkhā)* by remaining neutral whether others are helpful or harmful to any of these three.[2]

Great Bodhisattas are of three types:[3] (1) those in whom wisdom *(paññā)* is predominant, (2) those in whom faith *(saddhā)* is predominant, and (3) those in whom energy *(viriya)* is predominant. For the first type, the preparation requires four incalculables and one hundred thousand aeons. The second type

[1] See *Treatise*, pp. 312f.
[2] See *Treatise*, pp. 313f.
[3] See *Treatise*, pp. 325f.

works for eight incalculables and one hundred thousand aeons. The third type, to which Bodhisatta Metteyya belongs, works for sixteen incalculables and one hundred thousand aeons.[1] These three types are also explained by reference to the degree of energy they put forth, or again, by reference to the degree to which they develop the mental factors that bring emancipation to maturity *(vimuttiparipācaniyā dhammā)*.

These three types of Great Bodhisattas are determined by how much they have developed the perfections when they make the aspiration to become a Teaching Buddha. At the time they aspire to become a Teaching Buddha, they will already have prepared to attain final Nibbāna, Arahatship.[2] They will be at the point where they could, if they so wished, become Arahats (1) through a condensed teaching of less than three lines *(ugghaṭitaññū)*, (2) through an elaborated teaching of less than four lines *(vipañcitaññū)*, or (3) through further training amounting to hearing four lines *(neyya)*. According to the commentary on the Anāgatavaṃsa,[3] those in whom wisdom is predominant, which was the case for the Bodhisatta who became Buddha Gotama, would be able to understand a condensed teaching of less than three lines. Those in whom faith is predominant would understand a teaching of less than four lines. Those in whom energy is predominant, as is the case for Bodhisatta Metteyya, would understand on hearing four lines. This might seem to suggest that the future Buddha Gotama was more advanced than the future Buddha Metteyya when he made his resolve to become a Buddha. But the difference may be related to the fact that a Bodhisatta for whom energy is predomi-

---

[1] This is mentioned in Dvp, p. 133.

[2] CSM, pp. 130f. (in the discussion of "cause").

[3] In an unpublished passage. This is mentioned by Sayadaw U Vicittasārābhivaṃsa in his *Mahābuddhavaṅ* (Yangon: Sāsana Council, 1977), pp. 6-10 (he quotes as his source: Ashin Thilawuntha [Sīlavaṃsa], *Pāramī-kaṅ-pyo*).

nant develops the perfections four times as long as a Bodhisatta for whom wisdom is predominant.

There are many conditions associated with the resolve to become a Teaching Buddha.[1] The aspiration *(abhinīhāra)* is: "Crossed over I would cause (others) to cross over, released I would cause (others) to be released, tamed I would cause (others) to be tamed, calmed I would cause (others) to be calmed, comforted I would cause (others) to be comforted, completely quenched I would cause (others) to be completely quenched, Awakened I would cause (others) to be Awakened, purified I would cause (others) to be purified."

There are eight qualifications for the man who is to become a Great Bodhisatta to be sure that his aspiration will succeed:[2]

(1) He must be a human being *(manussatta)*, as this is the plane in which Buddhas arise.
(2) He must be a male *(liṅgasampatti)*, for only a man can become a Buddha.
(3) He must have achieved the necessary conditions supporting Buddhahood, in other words, the cause *(hetu)*, which means that at the time of the aspiration he was prepared to attain Arahatship.
(4) He must see the Teacher *(satthāradassana)*, as the aspiration can only be successful if made in the presence of a living Buddha. Only a Teaching Buddha can see the capability of the person making the aspiration and what will work out in the future.
(5) He must have gone forth *(pabbajjā)* either as a bhikkhu or as an ascetic who believes in the doctrines of volitional actions and the moral effectiveness of action.

---

[1] See *Treatise*, pp. 267-270.
[2] See CSM, pp. 132-134.

(6) He must have achieved the noble qualities *(guṇa-sampatti)* which come with highly developed control over the mind. Only then will he be able to investigate the ten perfections that he will need to develop.
(7) He must possess great dedication *(adhikāra)*. He will be so devoted he would give his life for a Buddha.
(8) And he must have a strong desire *(chandatā)*, a wholesome desire, if he is to develop the mental factors which make for Buddhahood.

The aspiration has one of four conditions *(paccaya)*: the man is inspired because (1) he sees a Teaching Buddha, or (2) he hears of the great power of a Teaching Buddha, or (3) he hears the Doctrine of a Teaching Buddha being taught and the powers of a Buddha explained, or (4) he is a man of lofty temperament and noble disposition. Bodhisatta Metteyya comes under the second condition, as we shall see.

The aspiration has four causes *(hetu)*:

(1) The Great Bodhisatta has already fulfilled his duties under former Buddhas and acquired the supporting conditions *(upanissaya)* for fulfilling his task. These supporting conditions create a clear distinction between the Great Bodhisatta and the beings intent on becoming Awakened as disciples or Pacceka Buddhas. Great Bodhisattas are endowed with lucid faculties and lucid knowledge, while the others are not. He practises for the welfare and happiness of many, out of compassion for the world, for the good, welfare, and happiness of Devas and men, while the others practise mainly for their own welfare. He applies skilfulness to his practice through his ability to create opportunities to benefit others and through his skill in distinguishing what is and what is not possible, while the others lack this ability and skill.

(2) He is by nature compassionate, ready to give his own body and life to alleviate the suffering of others.
(3) He is willing to struggle and strive for a long time, despite the great hardships he will encounter.
(4) He relies on good friends who restrain him from evil and establish him in what is good.

Finally, the aspiration is based on four powers *(bala):* (1) internal power *(ajjhattika-bala)*, (2) external power *(bāhira-bala)*, (3) the power of the supporting conditions *(upanissaya-bala)*, and (4) the power of effort *(payoga-bala)*. The internal power is the longing or undeviating inclination for supreme Awakening based on his personal ideals and reverence for the Dhamma. The external power is this same longing based on consideration of others. Through developing the supporting conditions, he has the power of this longing. And the power of effort means he is endowed with the appropriate effort for attaining supreme Awakening. His effort will be thorough and he will persevere in his work.

The Great Bodhisattas are confirmed in their aspiration by many Buddhas. A sixteenth-century Pāḷi text from Thailand[1] says that Bodhisatta Metteyya received his prediction of future Buddhahood from Buddha Mahutta. This would presumably be the first prediction for him. This text also gives details of the period during which the Bodhisatta who became Buddha Gotama made a mental resolve to become a Teaching Buddha. This is shown to be his preparation for the life in which he received his first sure prediction. Bodhisatta Metteyya is mentioned as being associated with him in two of these lives: as his leading disciple when he was a religious teacher[2] and as his chaplain (named Sirigutta) when he was King Atideva.[3]

---

[1] Jinakālamālī *(Epochs of the Conqueror)*.
[2] *Epochs*, pp. 5f.
[3] *Epochs*, pp. 8f.

The story of one occasion when Bodhisatta Metteyya made an aspiration and when the perfection which is strongest for him is illustrated is told in Pāḷi texts which were written down after the compilation of the Canon.[1] The story of Bodhisatta Metteyya's aspiration was told to the leading disciple Ven. Sāriputta when he was residing near Sāvatthi in the Pubbārāma, the monastery offered by the laywoman Visākhā.

Long ago, Bodhisatta Metteyya was the Wheel-Turning Monarch Saṅkha in the city of Indapatta in the Kuru country. This large city resembled a city of the Devas. Wheel-Turning Monarchs reign over the whole earth and have seven great treasures: a great wheel, an elephant, horse, gem, wife, householder, and adviser. Saṅkha lived in a seven-storey palace made of the seven kinds of gems. This palace rose up out of the earth through the power of his merit. Saṅkha led others to follow the path leading to rebirth in the higher planes of existence, and he administered justice with impartiality.

After Saṅkha became a Wheel-Turning Monarch, there arose the Buddha Sirimata.[2] Whenever a Bodhisatta is to be born in his last life, there is a Buddha proclamation a thousand years before.[3] Brahmās of the Pure Abodes (Suddhāvāsa) travel throughout the world of men and proclaim: "A thousand years from now, a Buddha will arise in the world." King Saṅkha must have heard of this proclamation, for one day, as he sat on his golden throne under the royal white umbrella, he said, "A long time ago there was a proclamation that a Buddha would be born. I will turn over the place of Wheel-Turning Monarch to whoever knows of the Triple Gem, to whoever points out to me the gems of the Buddha, the Dhamma, and the Saṅgha, as well as

---

[1] Dbk (see also pp. 391-413 of the next text), and Dbu.

[2] There does not seem to be any information as to when this Buddha lived. He would have lived before the twenty-four Buddhas under whom the Bodhisatta who became Buddha Gotama made his resolutions.

[3] See *Illus.*, p. 131.

the Dispensation. I will go to see the Supreme Buddha." Buddha Sirimata was residing at that time only sixteen leagues from Saṅkha's capital city. Among the sāmaṇeras (novices) in the Saṅgha, there was a boy who came from a poor family. His mother was a slave, so the sāmaṇera went to the city to seek wealth in order to set his mother free. When the people saw him, they thought he was a Yakkha, or ogre, so they threw sticks at him. Afraid, he went to the palace and stood before the king. "Who are you, young man?" the king asked.

"I am called a sāmaṇera, O great king," the sāmaṇera answered.

"Why do you call yourself a sāmaṇera?"

"Because, O great king, I do no evil, I have established myself in moral conduct, and thus I lead the holy life. Therefore I am called a sāmaṇera."

"Who gave you that name?"

"My teacher, O great king."

"What is your teacher called, young man?"

"My teacher is called a bhikkhu, O great king."

"Who gave your teacher the name 'bhikkhu,' young man?"

"O great king, my teacher's name was given by the priceless gem of the Saṅgha."

Full of joy, King Saṅkha rose from his throne and prostrated himself at the feet of the sāmaṇera. And he asked, "Who gave the name to the Saṅgha?" "O great king, the Noble Supreme Buddha Sirimata gave the name to the Saṅgha." Hearing the word "Buddha," which is so difficult to hear in many hundreds of thousands of aeons, King Saṅkha fainted from joy. When he regained consciousness, he asked, "Venerable sir, where does the Noble Supreme Buddha Sirimata reside at present?"

And the sāmaṇera told him the Buddha was in a monastery called Pubbārāma, sixteen leagues away. King Saṅkha turned over the power of Wheel-Turning Monarch to the sāmaṇera. He gave up his kingdom and a great number of relatives. Filled with joy at the thought of seeing the Buddha, he started walking to the north towards the Pubbārāma. The first day, the soles of his feet split open, for they were very tender due to his luxurious upbringing. On the second day, his feet began to bleed. He was unable to walk on the third day, so he went on his hands and knees. On the fourth day, his hands and feet bled, so he determined to continue on his chest. The joy of the possibility of seeing the Buddha enabled him to overcome his great suffering and pain.

Buddha Sirimata surveyed the world with his All-knowing Knowledge and seeing the power of the effort *(viriya-bala)* of the king, the Buddha thought, "This Wheel-Turning Monarch Saṅkha is surely a seed, a Buddha-sprout *(Buddhaṅkura-bījo)*. He undertakes great pain because of me. Indeed, I should go to him." By his psychic powers, the Buddha hid his great splendour and went disguised as a young man in a chariot. He went to where Saṅkha was and blocked his path in order to test the power of his effort.

"You there!" Buddha Sirimata said to King Saṅkha, "go back on your chest! I am going down this road in my chariot." But King Saṅkha refused, saying he was on his way to see the Buddha. The Buddha in disguise invited the king to get into his chariot, saying that is where he was going. On the way, the Deva maiden Sujātā came down from the Tāvatiṃsa heaven, and taking the form of a young girl, offered food. The Buddha had it given to Saṅkha. Then Sakka, in the form of a young man, came down from the Tāvatiṃsa heaven and gave water. As a result of the divine food and water, all King Saṅkha's ailments disappeared.

When they arrived at Pubbārāma, the Buddha sat on his seat in the monastery, assuming his true appearance with the rays of six colours shining forth. When the king went in and saw the Buddha, he again lost consciousness. After a while, he came to himself, approached the Buddha, and paid his respects.

"Venerable sir," he requested, "protector of the world, refuge of the world, teach me one (point of the) doctrine which may calm me when I have heard it." "Very well," the Buddha said, "listen." The Buddha reviewed the Doctrine of Nibbāna and taught the king a discourse concerning Nibbāna. This aroused reverence for the Doctrine in the king, but after hearing only a little of the Doctrine, he requested the Buddha, "Please stop, Blessed One. Do not teach me any more." He said this because he thought to himself that he would not have a gift worthy of what the Buddha taught him if he heard any more.

"Indeed, venerable sir," the king said, "of all the doctrines taught, the Blessed One has pointed out Nibbāna, which is the highest. So, of all the parts of my body, I will pay homage to your Doctrine with my head." He began to sever his neck with his fingernails and said, "Venerable Buddha Sirimata, you go[1] to the deathless first; through the gift of my head, I will afterwards go to Nibbāna. Having said just these few words, I pay homage to the doctrine of Nibbāna. Now, may this be the means for (my attaining) omniscience." And saying this, he finished severing his head with his fingernails.

King Saṅkha's predominant characteristic was his great energy *(viriya)*. This is shown through his overcoming the difficulties in going to see Buddha Sirimata. His effort was so strong, the Buddha realized that he was a Great Bodhisatta. Other perfections are also illustrated in this story. He gives away his position of Wheel-Turning Monarch. Even before hearing of the Buddha, he set the example of leading a moral life leading to higher rebirths. As a just king, he would show his wisdom, patience, truthfulness, loving kindness, and equanimity. Once he hears of the Buddha, he renounces his kingdom and family, giving up the highest position that can be attained by a human being. And great resolution worked together with his energy.

---

[1]Reading *yātha* with the Martini ed. (p. 395 and variant reading p. 306) for *yāva* in the Pali Text Society ed. (p. 127).

The final action of King Saṅkha is the gift of his head to the Buddha. This may seem strange, but it is explained in the text by the fact that the Buddha had taught him one aspect of the Doctrine concerning Nibbāna, the highest goal. King Saṅkha cannot find any other gift worthy of Nibbāna, so he resolves to offer his own head. In the Pāḷi commentaries,[1] it is said that only giving their own limbs or their life makes Great Bodhisattas exult when they give. Joy arises when they give such gifts and they experience no contrariety of mind. So we can see that such gifts are beyond ordinary people, and we need not feel that we should make such sacrifices ourselves.

During the time of Buddha Gotama, the Great Bodhisatta who is to be the next Buddha was a bhikkhu named Ajita.[2] According to the commentary on the Anāgatavaṃsa, Ajita was the son of King Ajātasattu and Queen Kañcanadevī.[3] Prince Ajita had five hundred attendants, and when he reached the age

[1]See CSM, p. 215.

[2]Dbk, p. 54.

[3]We base the following account on the information in Dipeyin Sayadaw's *Anāgatavaṃsa*. See also: Dbk, p. 54; Sylvain Levi, "Maitreya le consolateur," *Etudes d'orientalisme publiées par le Musée Guimet à la memoire de Raymonde Linossier* (1932), Vol. II, p. 366 (his information is based on a Pāḷi text from Thailand, Paṭhamasambodhi); and George Cœdès, "Une vie indochinoise du Bouddha: la Paṭhamasambodhi," *Mélanges d'indianiste à la memoire de Louis Renou* (1968), pp. 217-227. According to Dvp, Chapter 31 (Pāḷi, pp. 125-127, French, pp. 132-134), Ajita was from a prosperous family in Saṅkassa. This text says that Bodhisatta Metteyya had already fulfilled the perfections for sixteen incalculables and a hundred thousand aeons when he was born as a human during the time of Buddha Gotama. His family lived at the gate of the city Saṅkassa (Saṅkhassa in the French ed.). It was here that the Buddha descended from the Tāvatiṃsa Deva world after teaching the Abhidhamma. On this occasion he asked Ven. Sāriputta a question which none of the other disciples were able to answer in order to show that the chief disciple understood the Doctrine better than any of the other disciples (see *Buddhist Legends*, III, 54-56). When the Great Bodhisatta heard Ven. Sāriputta's answer, he was very pleased. Seeing the pleasing appearance of the Buddha and hearing him teach the Doctrine, Ajita was drawn to become a bhikkhu. (The French translation of this passage is slightly inaccurate.)

of sixteen, the king asked his son to inherit the Buddha's heritage. The Prince agreed, so the king took him to the Veḷuvana Monastery in great pomp and splendour along with his five hundred attendants. Prince Ajita was ordained as a novice, and because of his serenity, calmness, and wisdom he was much respected. Later he was ordained as a bhikkhu. The Buddha took him when he went from Rājagaha to Kapilavatthu to reside in the Nigrodhārāma Monastery.

While they were residing at that monastery, Mahā-Pajāpatī-Gotamī came one day with two special cloths to be presented to the Buddha for use as robes. She had planted the cotton seeds herself and did all the necessary work up to the time the robes were finished. The account of the gift of the cloths is found in the Majjhima-nikāya.[1] There, the Buddha refused three times to accept the robes offered by Mahā-Pajāpatī-Gotamī and suggested that she offer them to the Saṅgha with the Buddha at its head. Ven. Ānanda approached the Buddha, suggesting he should accept the cloths. The Buddha then gave the discourse on the analysis of offerings.

No other details are given in the Pāḷi Canon or Ācariya Buddhaghosa's commentary on this discourse. In the commentary on the Anāgatavaṃsa, it is said that the Buddha accepted one robe for himself and instructed his step-mother to offer the second one to the Saṅgha. But not one of the eighty leading disciples came forward to accept that robe. Eventually, Ven. Ajita thought to himself that the Buddha had told his step-mother to give the robe to the Saṅgha for her benefit, so he bravely got up like a king of the lions in the midst of the Saṅgha and accepted the robe. There was some disappointment and much talk about how an unknown bhikkhu could accept the robe when none of the leading disciples had taken it. Realizing the situation and in order to dispel any doubts, the Buddha said, "Do not say this

[1] Suttanta No. 142 (MLS, III 300-305).

bhikkhu is an ordinary bhikkhu. He is a Bodhisatta who will be the coming Buddha Metteyya." Then the Buddha took the bowl that had been given to him shortly after his Awakening by the world's four Guardian Devas and threw it into the air. None of the eighty leading disciples could retrieve it, but Ven. Ajita understood that the Buddha intended for him to show his psychic powers, so he brought back the bowl. Then Ven. Ajita took the cloth he had accepted and put it in the Buddha's Perfumed Chamber as a canopy under the ceiling, making the aspiration that this act of generosity might result in his having a canopy made of seven gems and with hangings made of gold, silver, coral, and pearls measuring twelve leagues when he becomes a Buddha.[1] The Buddha smiled after this and Ven. Ānanda asked why he had smiled. The Buddha replied, "Ānanda, the bhikkhu Ajita will become the Buddha Ariya Metteyya in this Auspicious Aeon." Then he remained silent, enjoying the fruits of Arahatship. The first chief disciple, Ven. Sāriputta, who knew the assembled bhikkhus wished to hear more information, requested the Buddha give a discourse about the coming Buddha. And the Buddha gave the account in the Anāgatavaṃsa.[2]

The prediction concerning Metteyya is found in the Pāḷi Canon,[3] but the details concerning the future Buddha will be

---

[1]The account in the Paṭhamasambodhi differs somewhat (see Sylvain Levi, "Maitreya," p. 366). In this account, Ajita is still a novice, the newest member of the Saṅgha. He is given both of the robes and uses the second one by tearing it up to make garlands to hang from the border of the canopy. After having done all this, Ajita makes a vow to become a Teaching Buddha and Buddha Gotama then gives his sure prediction. The details concerning the robe and the sure prediction are also found in Dvp (Pāḷi, p. 126).

[2]The Dhamek Stupa at Sarnath is said to be the place where the Buddha predicted the coming of Buddha Metteyya (Devapriya Valisinha, *Buddhist Shrines in India* [Colombo: The Maha Bodhi Society of Ceylon, 1948], p. 70; quoted in Sujata Soni, *Evolution of Stupas in Burma* [Delhi: Motilal Banarsidass, 1991], pp. 50, 87.

[3]D, No. 26 (DB, III, 72-74; TS, pp. 364-368).

given in a separate talk. The Dasavatthu goes on to say that from the time of the sure prediction, the Bodhisatta taught a large number of bhikkhus, explaining the whole Canon and helping them to increase their insight and to attain the knowledge of adaptable patience. At the end of that life, he was reborn in a Deva world. But there is a reference to at least one other human life as he should have a life in which he is generous in the way the Bodhisatta Vessantara was.[1] After that life, he should be reborn in the Tusita Deva world, where all Great Bodhisattas reside before their final birth. According to the Cūḷavaṃsa, the Bodhisatta would have other human births.[2]

When Ācariya Buddhaghosa went from India to Sri Lanka to consult the commentaries on the Pāḷi Canon, he was given two verses to comment on as a test. The result was the Visuddhimagga *(The Path of Purification)*. The Devas, in order to convince the people of his greatness, hid the text twice so that Ācariya Buddhaghosa had to copy it twice. When the copies were compared with the original, no deviations were found. The Saṅgha then exclaimed, "Without a doubt this is Metteyya!" The Visuddhimagga is especially important for those practising the Buddha's Teachings. Sayagyi U Ba Khin considered this work the most important single work explaining true Buddhist meditation.

In another Pāḷi text that is not part of the Canon, there is a description of Metteyya in the Tusita world.[3] He is said to go to the Cūlāmaṇi shrine in the Tāvatiṃsa Deva world to pay respects to the hair cut off by the Bodhisatta Siddhattha when he made the great renunciation and to relics brought there by the

---

[1]Sayagyi U Ba Khin interpreted this passage to mean that the generosity would consist mainly of the gift of the Dhamma (see above, p. 4).

[2]See Vol. I, 22-25 (Ch. XXXVII, verses 215-246). This passage is quoted by Ven. Ñāṇamoli in the introduction of his translation, *The Path of Purification* (pp. xxi-xxii).

[3]Sīh, Chapter III (Pāḷi, pp. 8-12; French, second pagination, pp. 10-14).

Deva king Sakka after the death of Buddha Gotama. The Bodhisatta Metteyya is described as being surrounded by a host of Devas and Devīs. Four Devī maidens in particular are described as having beautiful complexions, halos, ornaments, and clothes, one of a shining colour, one red, one dark gold, and the fourth, golden.

The main point of this text is that beings who wish to encounter the coming Buddha and attain Awakening under him should act accordingly. Bhikkhus should not create a schism in the Saṅgha. The five heinous actions which inevitably lead to rebirth in the lower worlds should be avoided. In addition to not creating a schism, these include not killing one's father, one's mother, or an Arahat. The fifth point, not drawing the blood of a Buddha, of course, is no longer possible. Other actions to be avoided are destroying pagodas *(thūpas)* or breaking Bodhi trees. Bodhisattas should not be killed. One should not be stingy or tell lies. In one of the texts about Buddha Gotama's description of the ten future Buddhas,[1] the following positive actions are said to be necessary if those who encounter this Buddha Dispensation wish to meet Buddha Metteyya: they must give gifts *(dāna)*, observe morality *(sīla)*, and develop mental control—that is to say, meditation *(bhāvanā)*.

Those of us today who are practising the Teachings of the Buddha should try to advance ourselves as far as possible. Some people may be able to become Ariyas here and now. People who have not developed the perfections required for such attainments or who have made an aspiration under a former Buddha to meet Buddha Metteyya will need to make a maximum effort in order not to miss this opportunity or in order to gain the maximum benefits. We should not just assume that we are meant to defer Awakening until we meet the next Buddha. Ācariya Buddhaghosa gives the example of Elder Mahā-Saṅgharakkhita who

[1] Dbu, p. 344.

needed a reminder in order not to miss his opportunity to attain Arahatship, for he had mistakenly thought he should wait until the next Buddha.[1] Meditators who become Ariyas aside from Arahats may eventually go to the Brahmā worlds of the Pure Abodes (Suddhāvāsa), and there they may live long enough to meet the coming Buddha.[2] So we should all make our best effort in this life.

---

[1] See *The Path of Purification*, Chapter I,135.

[2] See DB II, 39-41 (D, No. 14). Those who attain the third stage of Awakening (Non-Returners) can live in the Pure Abodes (Suddhāvāsa) of the Brahmā worlds long enough to encounter more than one Buddha. Buddha Gotama recounts meeting Brahmās in the Pure Abodes who confirm for him events that he recalls from the time of former Buddhas (see D, No. 14 [DB, II 4-41, especially pp. 39-41]).

BUDDHA ARIYA METTEYYA

Dwell, bhikkhus, with yourselves as an island, with yourselves as a refuge, with no one else as a refuge; with the Doctrine as an island, with the Doctrine as a refuge, with no other [doctrine] as a refuge.

And how, bhikkhus, does a bhikkhu dwell with himself as an island, with himself as a refuge, with no one else as a refuge; with the Doctrine as an island, with the Doctrine as a refuge, with no other [doctrine] as a refuge?

Here (in this Teaching), bhikkhus, a bhikkhu lives, contemplating the body in the body, contemplating the sensations in the sensations, contemplating the consciousness in the consciousness, contemplating mental objects in mental objects, ardent, attentive, mindful, having removed covetousness and discontent with regards to the world. Thus, bhikkhus, does a bhikkhu dwell with himself as an island, with himself as a refuge, with no one else as a refuge; with the Doctrine as a refuge, with no other [doctrine] as a refuge.

Dīgha-nikāya III 58, 77

This quotation begins the Discourse of the Lion's Roar on the Turning of the Wheel in which the Buddha describes the coming of the next Buddha, Metteyya.[1] The Buddha first

[1] D III 58-79, translated in DB III 59-76, TS 347-370, THIH 395-405. Miss Horner seems to overlook this when she says that there is no mention in the Canon or Commentaries that Buddha Gotama made a declaration of future Buddhahood for Metteyya (CB xvi).

describes the ideal conditions that existed on earth long ago when there was a succession of seven Wheel-Turning Monarchs. Eventually, a king reigned who neglected to provide for the poor. As a consequence, theft arose in the world. Gradually, people became more and more immoral and killed others. Because of this, their life span declined from eighty thousand years to forty thousand years. Then people began to tell lies, and the human life span declined to twenty thousand years. Next, malicious speech became prevalent, and the life span decreased to ten thousand years. Then sexual misconduct became prevalent, with the result that people lived for five thousand years. Harsh speech and frivolous talk became prevalent, and people lived for two and a half thousand years and two thousand years respectively. With the advent of covetousness and ill will, the life span declined to one thousand years. When people began to entertain wrong beliefs, their life span decreased to five hundred years. Then three things became rampant: incest, unnatural greed, and homosexuality.[1] As a result, the human life span decreased to two hundred and fifty years and two hundred years. Then there was a lack of filial duty towards parents, failure to fulfil duties towards religious leaders *(samaṇas* and *brāhmaṇas*), and failure to respect community leaders; and the life span decreased to one hundred years. This was the human life span at the time of Buddha Gotama. When the life span is shorter than a hundred years, there can be no Buddha in the world.[2]

The Buddha explained that immorality will continue to increase and the human life span will continue to decrease until it is only ten years. Girls will be married at five years of age. At that time, people who have no respect for their parents, for religious leaders, or for community leaders will be honoured and praised. Promiscuity will be so common, human beings will be

---

[1]See also GS I 142, where the Buddha says that these three things were already prevalent in his day.

[2]See CSM 391.

like animals. Animosity, ill will, and hatred will be so strong, people will want to kill the members of their own family. There will be a seven-day war with great slaughter. But some people will hide for the seven days, and afterwards they will rejoice to see those who have survived. They will determine to stop killing, and their life spans will increase to twenty years. Seeing this, they will undertake to keep other moral precepts, and gradually the human life span will increase again.

The Duration of the Sāsana of Buddha Gotama

During the period from the time of Buddha Gotama to the minimum life span, the Buddha's Dispensation *(Buddha-sāsana)* will disappear. When the Buddha agreed to create the Bhikkhunī Saṅgha, he told Ven. Ānanda that the Sāsana would last only half as long because of this. Instead of lasting one thousand years, it would last five hundred years. The commentary on the Abhidhamma text, Dhammasaṅgaṇī, says that when the First Buddhist Council convened by Ven. Mahā-Kassapa rehearsed the Pāḷi Canon, this made it possible for the Sāsana to endure for five thousand years.[1]

The commentaries on the Vinaya Piṭaka[2] and the Aṅguttara-nikāya[3] say that the eight important rules which the Buddha gave to the Bhikkhunī Saṅgha will make his Teachings last for five thousand years rather than five hundred. There will be one thousand years for Arahats who attain analytical insight, one thousand years for Arahats without those attainments, one thousand years for Non-Returners, one thousand years for Once-Returners, and one thousand years for Stream-Winners. After these five thousand years of penetration of the true Doctrine

[1] As 27, see *Expos.* 35.
[2] Sp 1291.
[3] Mp IV 136f.

(paṭivedha-saddhamma),[1] the accomplishment in the texts *(pariyatti-dhamma)* will remain. After the accomplishment in the texts disappears, the signs *(liṅga)* will continue for a long time.

In the commentary to the Theragāthā[2] the Sāsana is said to consist of five periods: (1) the age of deliverance *(vimutti-yuga)*, (2) the age of concentration *(samādhi-yuga)*, (3) the age of morality *(sīla-yuga)*, (4) the age of learning [the texts] *(suta-yuga)*, and (5) the age of generosity *(dāna-yuga)*. Ven. Dhammapāla says, concerning the disappearance of learning: "In a region where there is no purity of morality, accomplishment (in the texts) remains through taking up great learning, through the desire to acquire, etc. But when accomplishment in the summary [i.e., the Pātimokkha] is completely ended, it disappears. From that time on, only the mere signs *(liṅga)* remain. Then, having accumulated riches in various ways, they give away gifts *(dāna)*; this, truly, is the last right practice. Then, [the period starting] after the disappearance of learning is the last period *(pacchima-kāla)*. Others say that it is from the time of the disappearance of morality." According to the tradition in Myanmar, the Sāsana will last five thousand years. The five periods will occur twice. The first half of the Sāsana has just passed, with each of the five periods lasting five hundred years. We are now in the second half, when these periods will be repeated, each lasting for another five hundred years.

In the Anāgatavaṃsa commentary, the Buddha is said to preface the account of the future Buddha Ariya Metteyya by saying his own dispensation will disappear in five stages: (1) the disappearance of analytical insight *(paṭisambhidā)*, (2) the disappearance of the Paths and Fruition States, (3) the disappearance of the practice *(paṭipatti)*, (4) the disappearance of the texts *(pariyatti)*, and (5) the disappearance of the Saṅgha.

---

[1] Ven. Ledi Sayadaw (MB 169) calls these five thousand years the age of Ariyas (Noble Ones).

[2] Th-a III 89.

Other commentaries also speak in terms of five stages of disappearance *(antaradhāna)* of the Sāsana:[1] (1) First, there will be the disappearance of attainment *(adhigama)*, which would correspond to the age of deliverance. (2) The second disappearance is of the practice *(paṭipatti)*, which corresponds to the ages of concentration and morality. (3) The disappearance of accomplishment in the texts *(pariyatti)* is third and corresponds to the age of learning. (4) The fourth disappearance is of the signs *(liṅga)*. During this period, the only good action left is making gifts to those who wear a yellow strip of cloth around their necks, so this would correspond to the age of generosity. When this disappearance occurs, five thousand years will have passed.[2] After this period there occurs (5) the disappearance of the relics *(dhātu)*. When the relics no longer receive honour, they will assemble at the seat where the Buddha attained Awakening under the Great Bodhi tree. There, they will make an effigy of the Buddha and perform a marvel similar to the Twin Marvel and will teach the Doctrine. No human being will be present, only Devas from the ten thousand world systems will listen, and many of them will attain release. After that, the relics will be burned up without remainder.[3]

The Coming of Buddha Ariya Metteyya

In the discourse with which we began, the Buddha goes on to describe how morality among human beings grows stronger and stronger. As a result, their life span grows longer until it reaches eighty thousand years,[4] and at that time, Buddha Metteyya will come. Ācariya Buddhaghosa explains that the life span increases

[1] See the commentary on A (Mp I 87), Moh 201-203, and the extract from the Anāg commentary (JPTS, 1886, pp. 33-36; translated in BT 481-486).

[2] The number of years is mentioned only in the Anāg commentary.

[3] Some texts speak of three disappearances. See CPD under *antaradhāna* for references.

[4] Dbk 55/120 says 82,000 years.

to an incalculable number of years *(asaṅkheyya)* and then begins to decrease again until it reaches 80,000 years, for Buddhas arise only when the life span is decreasing.[1] A tradition in Myanmar says that Buddha Metteyya will live for 80,000 years and that the human life span will be 100,000 years, just as Buddha Gotama lived for eighty years when the human life span was one hundred years. No definite number of years is given for the period between Buddha Gotama and Buddha Metteyya. The Anāgatavaṃsa (verse 5) says Buddha Metteyya will arise ten million years later *(vassa-koṭiye)*, but the commentary[2] says this means after many hundreds of thousands times ten million years.[3]

This aeon *(kappa)* is an Auspicious Aeon *(baddha-kappa)*, which means that the maximum number of five Buddhas will arise in the same aeon. Some aeons are empty ones, meaning no Buddhas arise. In other types of aeons, one to four Buddhas arise. Buddha Gotama was the fourth Buddha in this Auspicious Aeon, so Metteyya will be the last Buddha in it. The commentary to the Buddhavaṃsa says that an Auspicious Aeon is very difficult to encounter. Those who are born in such aeons are usually rich in goodness and happiness. They usually have the three root conditions (of non-greed, non-hatred, and non-confusion) and destroy the defilements. Those with the two root conditions (of non-greed and non-hatred) are usually reborn in good planes of existence, and those with no root condition acquire one.[4] In another commentary,[5] it is said that during the

---

[1]Sv III 885f.

[2]JPTS, 1886, p. 41, n. 5.

[3]Dvp 125/132 says that after the human life span decreases to ten years, there will be seven intervening aeons *(sattantara-kappa)*, then the life span will increase to an incalculable, and when it has decreased again to 80,000 years, the next Buddha will arise.

[4]CSM 277.

[5]Spk III 390; cf. KS IV 60, n. 2.

time of Buddha Metteyya, the group of sensual pleasures will have little initial power (to distract).

The Birth of the Next Buddha

Many details concerning the coming Buddha can be assembled by combining Buddha Gotama's prediction in the Dīgha-nikāya,[1] the Anāgatavaṃsa,[2] the two versions of *The Ten Bodhisattas*,[3] and the Dasavatthuppakarana.[4] Further details can be added from the description by Buddha Gotama of the past Buddha Vipassī,[5] Ven. Ānanda's praise of the Buddha,[6] and the commentary on *The Chronicle of Buddhas*.[7]

Before his last rebirth, which is in the human world, each Bodhisatta resides in the Tusita Deva world. He is mindful and aware when he is reborn there and while he lives there. He lives there as long as his life span lasts. One thousand years before he is to be reborn as a human and become a Buddha, Devas or Brahmās go to the world of men and announce that a Buddha will arise. This is a Buddha tumult.[8]

When the time is right, he descends into his mother's womb,[9] mindful and aware. He is aware it is his last existence. At that time, there is an illimitable, splendid radiance throughout the universe. His mother is protected by four Devas during the

---

[1]D III 75-77 (DB III 72-74; TS 365-368).

[2]This "Chronicle of the Future" is entirely devoted to the next Buddha.

[3]Dbk 55f., 61/120f., 127f.; Dbu 298-302, 306/338-341, 344.

[4]Dvp 125-127/132-134.

[5]D II 1-54 (DB II 4-41) (Mahāpadāna Suttanta).

[6]M sutta n° 123 (MLS III 163-169).

[7]CSM 428-430.

[8]CSM 389 mentions three such tumults and says the four guardian Devas will make the announcement of a Buddha. *Illus.* 130f. mentions five tumults and says the Brahmās of the Suddhāvāsa Brahmā world announce a Buddha.

[9]According to Dbu he is conceived on the full-moon day of Āsāḷha (June-July).

gestation period. His mother does not break the five precepts during her pregnancy, and she is not attracted to any man. The mother is surrounded by all the pleasures of the five senses. She suffers from no illness, and she can see the Bodhisatta in her womb. He is seated cross-legged in the womb facing outward.

His mother gives birth in a standing position and in a forest. The Bodhisatta Metteyya will be born in the deer park at Isipatana.[1] The feet of the baby are placed in a golden cloth. He is received first by Devas and afterwards by men. Before his feet touch the ground, four Devas present him to his mother, saying, "Rejoice, lady, for mighty is the son that is born to you." He comes forth without any stain. Two showers of cool and warm water fall from the sky to bathe the mother and the Bodhisatta. He takes seven steps to the north, surveys the four quarters, and pronounces the lion's roar that he is supreme in the world. When he is born, an illimitable, splendid radiance is seen throughout the universe. Seven days after the birth of the Bodhisatta, his mother dies and is reborn in the Tusita Deva world.[2]

When Bodhisatta Metteyya is reborn in the human world, life on earth will be like life in a Deva world. Women will marry at the age of five hundred. There will only be three diseases: desire (to eat) *(icchā)*, sluggishness after eating *(anasana)*, and old age *(jarā)*.[3] India will have Ketumatī (present-day Baranasi) as its capital city. In addition, there will be 84,000 cities with 90,000 crores of princes.[4] India will extend for 100,000 leagues.[5] It will be without thorns, clear, with green grass. There will be grass

[1] According to Dvp 126/133.

[2] See Th-a I 502. From the Tusita world, she goes to the Tāvatiṃsa world to hear the Abhidhamma.

[3] The translation of the first two diseases is based on the commentary to D III 75 (Sv 855). Pj II 323 says these mean (1) the craving which is a wish to be a Deva *(Devapatthana-taṇhā)*, (2) hunger *(khudā)*, and (3) the decay of old age *(paripāka-jarā)*.

[4] Dbu 299/339.

[5] Anāg vv 33-42.

which is four inches high and soft as cotton. The climate will always be good. The rains will be even, and the winds will be neither too hot nor too cold. The rivers and ponds will not lack water. There will be white sand that is not rough, the size of peas and beans. The country will be like an adorned garden. The villages will be close together, full of people, without interval.

The people will be tranquil, safe, and free from danger. They will be happy and joyful, enjoying festivals. They will have plenty to eat and drink. India will be delightful, like Āḷaka-mandā, the capital city of the Kurus. The capital city of India,[1] Ketumatī, will be twelve leagues long and seven leagues wide.[2] The city will have beautiful lotus ponds, full of water that is fragrant, clear, clean, cool, and sweet. The ponds will be accessible to people at all times. There will be seven rows of palm trees and walls of seven colours, made of jewels, will surround the city.

In squares at the gates of the city, there will be shining wish-fulfilling trees: one blue, one yellow, one red, and one white.[3] Celestial adornments and ornaments as well as all sorts of wealth and possessions will be hanging on the trees.

The Wheel-Turning Monarch Saṅkha

At this time, there will be a Wheel-Turning Monarch named Saṅkha. [4] In a past life, he and his father had made a hut for a Pacceka Buddha. They had him stay there for the three months of the rains retreat and then gave him three robes. In the same

---

[1] Anāg vv 8, 15-20.

[2] Dbu 299/338 says one league wide.

[3] According to Dbu 106/344 a wish-fulfilling tree will spring up through the merit of the seven-days walk made by the Bodhisatta in the past life when he went to see Buddha Sirimata.

[4] Not to be confused with the Bodhisatta Saṅkha. According to Dbu, the future Saṅkha is a Deva named Mahā-Naḷakāra (cf. D-t 43). Naḷakāra was the name of Mahā-Panāda in the Tāvatiṃsa Deva world (Ja IV 318-323).

way, they had seven Pacceka Buddhas stay in the hut. The father and son[1] were reborn in the Tāvatiṃsa Deva world, and Sakka requested that the father be reborn in the human world as Prince Mahā-Panāda. The architect for the Devas, Vissakamma, built a palace for Mahā-Panāda. During the time of Buddha Gotama, Mahā-Panāda was the Elder Bhaddaji, who, on one occasion, raised up the Mahā-Panāda palace from the bottom of the Ganges. The palace still waits there for the future Saṅkha, who was the son that gave to the Pacceka Buddhas in the past.[2]

When Saṅkha becomes the Wheel-Turning Monarch, he will raise up the Mahā-Panāda palace which will serve as his palace in the centre of Ketumatī. The palace is described as resplendent with many jewels, so bright that it is hard to look at.[3] He will possess the seven treasures of a Wheel-Turning Monarch: the wheel, elephant, horse, gem, wife, householder, and adviser.[4]

Through the merit of Saṅkha, there will be a square in the middle of the city with four halls facing the four directions with wishing trees. Hanging from the trees there will be all sorts of fine garments, drums, and jewellery.

Through the merit of the people at that time, there will be rice that grows without being cultivated. It will be pure, sweet-smelling, and the grains will be ready-husked. The residents of

---

[1]The account in Ja No. 489 says the father became Mahā-Panāda. Sv III 856 says it was the son and that the father is still in the Deva worlds. D-ṭ 43 gives his name as Naḷakāra ("the basket maker") which would mean both father and son had this name in the Deva worlds. Dvp (119-127/126-134) gives their names as Nāva-khuddhaka-Naḷakāra (or Cula-Naḷakāra), meaning "the younger Naḷakāra," and Jeṭṭhaka-Naḷakāra (or Jeṭṭha-Naḷakāra), meaning "the older Naḷakāra," so that here too it is the father who will be the future Saṅkha.

[2]Sv III 856f. says that the palace has not disappeared because of the meritorious act done by both the father and son in the past. Thus, it awaits the future king, Saṅkha, to be enjoyed by him.

[3]Anāg vv 12-14. Cf. Th vv 163-164.

[4]In Dvp (125/132) his career as a Wheel-Turning Monarch is described as following the pattern for other Monarchs (see DPPN II 1343ff.).

Ketumatī will have whatever they want. They will be very rich. They will wake up to the sound of drums and lutes. They will be exceedingly happy in both body and mind.[1]

King Saṅkha's palace will have 84,000 dancing girls.[2] He will have one thousand sons, valiant, of heroic forms, crushing enemy armies.[3] The eldest son[4] will be the king's adviser. The king will conquer the sea-girt land (of India) without violence, without a sword, but rather by righteousness.

The Career of Bodhisatta Metteyya

The Bodhisatta will be the son of the Wheel-Turning Monarch's head priest, Subrahma, and his wife, Brahmavatī.[5] He will be named Ajita, and he will bear the thirty-two marks and eighty minor marks that are common to Buddhas and Wheel-Turning Monarchs.[6] He will lead the household life for eight thousand years. He will have four palaces named:[7] Sirivaḍḍha, Vaḍḍhamāna, Siddhattha, and Candaka. He will have 100,000 dancing girls.[8] His wife will be Candamukhī[9] and his son will be named Brahmavaddhana.

---

[1] Anāg vv 27-32.

[2] Dbu 300/338. Th v 164: "6000 musicians danced there."

[3] D III 75 (DB III 73). This is a common feature to all Wheel-Turning Monarchs, see Sn p. 106 (GD 96).

[4] He will have the same name as the Bodhisatta in that life: Ajita (according to Dbu 300/338).

[5] Also mentioned in Vism chap. XIII, 127 and As 415 (Expos. 525). Dvp (126/133) gives the mother's name as Pajāpatī.

[6] For the list of the 32 marks, see D I 17-19 (DB I 1416). The 80 minor marks are given in the introduction to Dbk.

[7] This is the only case in which a Bodhisatta is said to have four rather than three palaces. As each of the three palaces were used for one of the three seasons, we can surmise that there will be four seasons during the time of the next Buddha. Dbu (300/339), and Dvp (126/133) mention only three palaces.

[8] Dbu (300/339) says 700,000.

[9] According to Dvp (126/132) she will be the chief consort out of 1,000 wives.

Bodhisattas decide to give up household life after they have seen the four signs (an old man, a sick man, a dead man, and a contented man who has gone forth from lay life) and after a son is born to them. They put on the yellow robe and engage in striving. The Bodhisatta Metteyya will go forth in one of his palaces. Accompanied by his followers, he will fly through the air in the palace and go to the Nāga tree, which will be his Bodhi tree. He will engage in striving for seven days, which is the minimum period.

There is a detailed account of these events in the Dasabodhisatta-uddesa:[1]

At the age of eight thousand years, the Bodhisatta will mount a chariot that resembles a glorious celestial palace and when going to the royal park, he will see the four signs. They will produce the knowledge of a sense of urgency. And he will long for the state of going forth. Then he will return and go up to his palace. His mind will be bent on the state of going forth. At that moment, that jewel palace will fly up by a path in the sky, and he will leap up into the sky, like the king of the golden water fowl, together with his followers.

Then the Devas of the ten thousand world systems will take flowers and honour him. The eighty-four thousand kings (of India), the people from the cities and from the countryside will honour him with perfume and flowers. The king of the Asuras will guard the palace. The king of the Nāgas will take (him) a precious gem, the king of the Supaṇṇas will take (him) a jewel necklace, the king of Gandhabbas will honour him with musical instruments and dancers. The Wheel-Turning Monarch, together with his consorts and followers, will go to the Bodhisatta.

By the power of the king and the power of the Great Being, all that crowd will be established in the state of going forth, and the people will rise into the sky with him and go [to the Bodhi

---

[1]Dbu 300/339f.

tree]. Then, the Mahā-Brahmā will take a sixty-league parasol and hold it [over them]. The Deva king Sakka will blow the Vijayuttara[1] conch shell. [The king of the Yāma Devas,] Suyāma, will take a yak's tail fan and honour him. [The king of the Tusita Devas,] Santusita, will hold a jewel fan. [The Gandhabba Deva,] Pañcasikha, will take his celestial lute Velupaṇḍa,[2] and play it. The [four Great Deva] Kings, swords in hand, will surround them on all four sides. All those Devas, all those people and Gandhabbas, all those Yakkhas, Nāgas, and Supaṇṇas, surrounding him in front, in back, and on both sides, will go with him. Surrounded by that crowd of Devas, women, etc., of great splendour and beauty, he [the Bodhisatta] will rise into the sky, [and then] descend near the Terrace of Awakening. At that moment, the Mahā-Brahmā will take the eight requisites [of an ascetic] created by his psychic powers and offer them to him. Then the Great Being will cut off the topknot of hair [on his head] and throw it up in the sky. He will take the eight requisites from the hands of the [Mahā-]Brahmā and go forth. For seven days he will make the Great Effort. And all that great crowd [of people] will follow the [example] of the Great Being in going forth.

The Nāga tree where the Bodhisatta will be Awakened is described[3] as being 120 cubits high with four (main) branches 120 or 130 cubits long. There will be 2,000 (minor) branches.[4] The tips of the branches will be bent, (constantly) moving, and will be continually in bloom with blossoms as big as wheels.

---

[1]Alternate reading: Vijjuttara.

[2]Usually named Beluva-paṇḍu-vīnā. PED defines *vīnā* as a lute, but translates as "flute" (sic) under the entries *paṇḍu* and *beluva*.

[3]Dvp 126f./134, Dbu 300f./340; Anāg vv 100-103.

[4]Dbu says that from the root to the extremity of the branches will be 200 feet plus 40 cubits. Anāg says the trunk will measure 2,000 cubits.

They will have a heavenly smell, full of pollen.[1] The perfume will spread around for ten leagues, both with and against the wind. The leaves will be a deep green in all seasons and the flowers will scatter on the people all around.

The Anāgatavaṃsa[2] describes the people who go forth with the Buddha, including the names of the most important people among them. He will be accompanied by a large group of people, including friends, ministers, and members of his family. There will be a fourfold army and an assembly of the four castes to go forth with him. There will be 84,000 princesses and 84,000 brahmans who are skilled in the Vedas. Among the 84,000 there will be the brothers Isidatta and Purāṇa; the twins of unlimited wisdom, Jātimitta and Vijaya; the householder Suddhika and the female disciple Suddhanā; the male disciple Saṅkha and the female disciple Saṅkhā;[3] the householder Saddara and the famous man Sudatta; and the husband and wife Visākha and Yasavatī. Many other citizens and people from the countryside of various social rank will go forth.

The spot on which the Bodhisattas attain Awakening is one of the four fixed places, so Metteyya will make his final bid for liberation on the same spot as all the past Buddhas—the present-day Buddha Gayā. On the day they attain Self-Awakening, Bodhisattas have a meal of milk-rice. They are seated on a spreading of grass. They use mindfulness of breathing as their preparation for developing insight and shatter the forces of Māra. They attain the three knowledges and the special qualities not shared by others, etc., while still seated in the cross-legged position. And they spend seven weeks near the Tree of Awakening after becoming Self-Awakened. The Anāgatavaṃsa commentary says that from the time he becomes Awakened, Ariya

[1] Anāg v 100 says the pollen (of each bloom) will be enough to fill a *nāḷi* measure.

[2] Vv 55-63.

[3] Alternate reading: Saṅgha and Saṅghā.

Metteyya will be known as the King of the Buddhas *(Buddha-rājā).*

Then the Mahā-Brahmā will request that Buddha Metteyya teach others the path to Nibbāna.

Buddha Metteyya will preach his first discourse, the Setting in Motion of the Wheel of the Doctrine, in Nāgavana ("The Elephant Grove").[1] The park is said to be in Isipatana near the city of Ketumatī.[2] He will be surrounded by an assembly extending one hundred leagues. A great many Devas will approach him at that time, and he will set free one hundred crores from their bondage.[3] This will be the first occasion when a great number of beings attain penetration *(abhisamaya)* into the Four Noble Truths.[4]

Then King Saṅkha will give his jewel palace to the Saṅgha with the Buddha at its head, and he will make a great donation to the poor, the needy, and beggars. Accompanied by his wife and 90,000 crores of people, the king will approach the Buddha. And all those 90,000 crores of people will be ordained with the words "Come, bhikkhu" *(ehi bhikkhu)*.[5] This will be the second penetration.

After that, the third penetration of 80,000 crores will take place when Devas and men approach the Buddha with a question concerning Arahatship.

---

[1]Dvp (126f./134) says it will be at the park in Isipatana near the city of Ketumatī. In this version, King Saṅkha is present for the First Sermon.

[2]CSM 429, but cf. CB xxii.

[3]Dvp (127/134) says an incalculable. Dbu (301/340) says 100 crores of humans and an unlimited number of Devas.

[4]The twenty-five Buddhas described in the Buddhavaṃsa (including Buddha Gotama) are said to have three "penetrations."

[5]In CSM (279), only Buddha Padumuttara is described as having "Ehi bhikkhus" in a "penetration." Many past Buddhas had such bhikkhus in assemblies.

There will be three assemblies *(sannipāta)* of Arahats.[1] The first will include 100,000 crores. This may be, as for many past Buddhas, at the time the Buddha recites the Pātimokkha on the full-moon day of Māgha to an assembly possessing four factors: (1) all the bhikkhus present are ordained with the "Come, bhikkhu" ordination, (2) all have the six types of higher knowledge, (3) all of them come without any previous announcement, and (4) the observance day *(uposatha)* is on the fifteenth (day in the bright fortnight).[2] The second assembly will be at the time the Buddha proclaims the "Invitation" at the end of the rainy season and will include 90,000 crores. For the third assembly, 80,000 crores of Arahats will accompany the Buddha when he goes in seclusion on the Gandhamādana slope of the Himavant mountain range. Otherwise, the Buddha Metteyya will continually be surrounded by 100,000 crores of those who have attained the six types of higher knowledge *(abhiññā)* and great psychic power.[3]

Buddha Gotama said[4] that just as he was accompanied by a Saṅgha of hundreds of bhikkhus when he wandered around,[5] Buddha Metteyya will be accompanied by thousands.

Buddha Metteyya will go through the countryside teaching the Doctrine, awakening many people.[6] Some will take the three refuges, some will be established in the five precepts, some will undertake the ten skilful actions. There will be some who become ordained, some who attain the four excellent Fruition States, some who will attain analytic insight into the Doctrine, some who will attain the eight excellent perfections, some the

---

[1]Buddhas generally have three assemblies, but Buddha Gotama and the three Buddhas before him had only one each (D I 2-7 [DB I 6f.]).

[2]Cf. CSM 180.

[3]Anāg v 83.

[4]D III 76 (DB III 74).

[5]The last detail is added by the commentary (Sv 856).

[6]This paragraph is based on Anāg vv 87-95.

three knowledges, and some the six types of higher knowledge. The Teachings of Buddha Metteyya will be widespread. Seeing people who are ready to be Awakened, he will go 100,000 leagues in a moment to cause them to be Awakened.

It is even said that Buddha Metteyya will quench the heat for beings reborn in the lower realms.[1] The first chief disciple will be the Wheel-Turning Monarch Saṅkha who will have the bhikkhu name of Asoka.[2] The second chief disciple will be Brahmadeva. The Buddha's attendant will be named Sīha. The chief women disciples among the bhikkhunīs will be Padumā and Sumanā. The chief lay attendants among the men will be Sumana[3] and Saṅgha;[4] among the women, Yasavatī and Saṅghā.[5]

Wherever he goes, Buddha Metteyya will be accompanied by a great company of Devas honouring him.[6] The Devas of the sense-sphere heavens will make necklaces which will be adorned by the kings of the Nāgas and Supaṇṇas. There will be eight garlands each of gold, silver, jewels, and coral. There will be many hundreds of banners hanging down. Awnings adorned with jewels will resemble the moon. They will be surrounded by nets of bells and jewelled garlands. They will scatter sweet-smelling flowers and different sorts of (perfumed) powder, both celestial and human. And there will be various types of cloth of many colours. Having faith in the Buddha, they will sport all around. And many marvels will take place through the power of

---

[1] Sīh III v 20.

[2] Names of the chief disciples are found in Anāg vv 97-99. The commentary in BN 630/862 gives the information concerning Saṅkha taking the bhikkhu name of Asoka.

[3] Alternate reading in BN 630/862: Suddhana.

[4] Alternate reading: Saṅkha.

[5] Alternate reading: Saṅkhā. These two pairs are identified as lay disciples in BN 630/862.

[6] Details in this paragraph are from Anāg vv 112-123.

Buddha Metteyya's merit. Seeing those marvels, many people will decide they would rather die than abandon him as their refuge. Many of them will attain Awakening, and those who do not will do good deeds which lead to heavenly worlds.

Several other details can be predicted for Buddha Metteyya as they are part of the list of thirty things that are true of all Buddhas:[1] he will live regularly at a monastery at Jetavana. His bed there will be on the same spot as those of past Buddhas. He will perform the Marvel of the Double at the gateway to the city of Sāvatthī. He will teach the Abhidhamma to his mother in the Tāvatiṃsa Deva world. He will descend from that Deva world at the gateway to the city of Saṅkassa.

He will lay down a rule of training whenever necessary. He will tell the story of one of his past lives (Jātaka) whenever necessary, and he will teach the Buddhavaṃsa *(The Chronicle of Buddhas)* to a gathering of his relatives.

Several details have to do with his day-to-day habits: he will give a friendly welcome to bhikkhus when they arrive. He will spend the rains retreat where he is invited to and will not leave without asking permission. Each day, he will carry out the duties to be performed before and after meals and for the three watches in the night.

Many details are given about the physical appearance of Buddha Metteyya.[2] He will be eighty-eight cubits[3] high. His chest will be twenty-five cubits in diameter.[4] There will be twenty-two cubits from the soles of his feet to the knees, from the knees to the navel, from the navel to the collar bone, and from the collar bone to the apex of his head. His arms will be

---

[1]CSM 428ff.

[2]Dbk 55/61, Dbu 301/340, Anāg vv 105-109.

[3]Miss Horner says that a cubit *(hattha)* is the distance between the elbow and the tip of the extended middle finger (CB xxii).

[4]Dbk says 25 cubits broad and 25 cubits lengthwise. Dbu says 25 cubits thick.

twenty-five cubits long.[1] The collar bones will be five cubits.[2] Each finger will be four cubits. Each palm will be five cubits. The circumference of the neck will be five cubits. Each lip will be five cubits.[3] The length of his tongue will be ten cubits. His elevated nose will be seven cubits. Each eye socket will be seven cubits. The eyes themselves will be five cubits. The Anāgatavaṃsa says[4] his eyelashes will be thick, that the eyes will be broad and pure, not winking day or night;[5] and that with his physical eye, he will be able to see large and small things all around for ten leagues without obstruction. The space between the eyebrows will be five cubits.[6] The eyebrows will be five cubits. Each ear will be seven cubits.[7] The circumference of his face will be twenty-five cubits.[8] The spiral of the protuberance on his head[9] will be twenty-five cubits.

Rays of six colours will radiate from his body and illumine the 10,000 world systems.[10] The major and minor marks will always be visible as countless hundreds of thousands of rays[11] that will shine in all directions for twenty-five leagues.[12] Through the merit acquired when the blood flowed from his head when he offered it to Buddha Sirimata, his radiance as a Buddha *(Buddha-pabhā)* will shine from the summit of the

---

[1]Dbu says 40 cubits.

[2]Dbu says from one shoulder to the other will be 25 cubits.

[3]Dbu says 15 cubits, but a variant reading gives 5.

[4]V 106.

[5]Usually given as a sign of a Deva or Yakkha.

[6]Dbu says 4.

[7]Dbu says 5.

[8]Dbk has "the circle of the face and ears" (trans.: "each auricle"). Dbk: *kaṇṇa-mukha-maṇḍalaṃ*; Dbu: *mukha-maṇḍalaṃ*.

[9]Dbu 301: *āvatta-uṇhīsaṃ*. This mark is not entirely clear as it seems an exceptionally high figure.

[10]Dbk 55/120, Dbu 301/340.

[11]Anāg v 109.

[12]Anāg v 107, Dbk 61/128.

world to the lowest of the hells, Avīci, and the offering of his head and the drops of blood will mean that the radiance from the hair between his eyebrows will be unlimited.[1]

People will not be able to distinguish night from day.[2] The only way they will know when it is night is through the sound of bird cries and the closing of the blossoms and leaves of lotuses and water lilies. They will know it is day by the cries of birds going to seek food and the opening of the flowers and leaves of lotuses and water lilies.[3]

Wherever Buddha Metteyya walks, lotuses will spring up for him to step on.[4] This is said to be the result of his great effort in the past life when he was King Saṅkha and went to Buddha Sirimata.[5] The main petals of the lotuses will be thirty cubits, and the minor petals, twenty-five. The stamens will be twenty cubits,[6] the pistils will be sixteen cubits, and they will be full of red pollen.[7]

But even Buddhas are subject to the law of impermanence. Eventually, Buddha Metteyya will attain final Nibbāna. All Buddhas have a meal with meat on the day of their final Nibbāna. Before their final Nibbāna, they will have accomplished 2,400,000 crores of attainments.[8] According to the Anāgatavaṃsa commentary, when Ariya Metteyya attains final Nibbāna,

---

[1]Dbu 306/344.

[2]According to Dbu (106/344) he will shine both day and night through the merit he acquired from the blood which flowed from his legs and feet when he went to see Buddha Sirimata in a past life.

[3]Dbk 120f./55, Dbu 301f./340.

[4]Details from Anāg vv 110f., Dbk 55/121, and Dbu 302/341.

[5]Dbk 61/128.

[6]Left out of the translation of Dbk (p. 55).

[7]Dbk translates "pollen of ten cubits" for *dasa-dasa-sampannā reṇū* which should perhaps mean "filled with tens (of loads) of pollen" (Dbu has *dasā-ḍasa-ammaṇa-reṇukā, ammaṇa* meaning "a load"). The size of an *ammaṇa* is not known precisely, but would be a large quantity.

[8]CSM 430.

he will not leave behind his human body (*vipāka-kammaja-rūpa*, "the body produced by the fruition [of volitional actions]"); he will enter the element of Nibbāna *(nibbāna-dhātu)* and no relics will remain. Although the poem says his dispensation will last for 180,000 years,[1] the commentary says it will continue for 380,000 years.

How to Meet Buddha Metteyya

The Dasabodhisatta-uddesa and Anāgatavaṃsa both give instructions on what people must do if they are to meet Buddha Metteyya. This is very important for all those who do not attain at least the first stage of Awakening during this Buddha Dispensation, for, as we have seen, Buddha Metteyya will be the last Buddha to arise in this world cycle. If a person does not attain Awakening in this world cycle, it will be extremely difficult to get another opportunity.

In the Dasabodhisatta-uddesa,[2] Buddha Gotama says to Ven. Sāriputta, "Not all men will see my physical body. If they encounter my Teachings *(sāsana)*, give gifts *(dāna)*, observe morality *(sīla)*, and cultivate development of the mind *(bhāvanā)*, through the fruit of that, they will be reborn in the time of Buddha Ariya Metteyya."

These three actions are the basis of meritorious action *(puñña)*.[3] Through these actions a person can be assured of rebirth in the higher planes of existence. Developing the mind leads to the temporary purity attained through the Jhāna states. But it can also lead to insight *(vipassanā)* and true liberation.

The Anāgatavaṃsa[4] gives more details. In order to meet Buddha Metteyya, people should put forth effort *(viriya)* and be

[1] Anāg v 134.
[2] 306/344.
[3] DB III 211.
[4] Vv 138-142.

firm *(daḷha)*, with agitated mind *(ubbigga-mānasa)*. We can surmise that "agitated mind" means the profound stirring of the mind or sense of urgency *(saṃvega)* that comes from realizing the urgent need to work for liberation. All those who do good deeds and who are vigilant—whether they are bhikkhus, bhikkhunīs, laymen, or laywomen—will be able to encounter the next Buddha. All those who pay great honour to the Buddha will see the auspicious assembly of Buddha Metteyya. The holy life *(brahma-cariya)* should be practised. Gifts *(dāna)* should be given. The Observance days *(uposatha)* should be kept. Loving kindness *(mettā)* should be carefully developed. By delighting in vigilance and meritorious actions, it will eventually be possible to make an end to misery *(dukkha)*.

Ven. Ledi Sayadaw[1] points out that it is necessary to make balanced effort in terms of good conduct *(caraṇa)* and right knowledge *(vijjā)* if one is to meet the next Buddha.

Right conduct means developing morality (*sīla)* and concentration *(samādhi)*. Knowledge means developing wisdom *(paññā)*. Right conduct can be compared to having sound limbs. Right knowledge can be compared to being able to see. If one or the other is missing, a person will be unsuccessful. A person may be generous and keep the permanent moral rules of the five precepts and the eight precepts on Observance days, but if the seeds of knowledge are not planted, that person may meet Buddha Metteyya but not be able to be Awakened. If only knowledge is developed, wrong conduct will mean that the chances of encountering the next Buddha will be slight, due to the intervening period (*antara-kappa)* between this Buddha Dispensation and the next one.

Examples of wrong conduct mentioned by Ven. Ledi Sayadaw are: not being generous, being poorly guarded in physical actions, being unrestrained in speech, and unclean in thought.

[1]MB 176-172. Cf. Vism, chap. VII, 30.

Such conduct will mean rebirth in the lower realms, either in the next life or in a future life. If people who act in this way do manage to be reborn in a higher world, their lack of generosity will mean they will encounter hardships, trials, and tribulations in making a living. Through not keeping the precepts, they are likely to meet with disputes, quarrels, anger, and hatred; and they will be susceptible to diseases and ailments. This will make it even harder to avoid actions leading to the lower worlds.

It may be possible, however, that a person today has already prepared in the past for attaining Awakening. If the right effort is made in this life, that person can reach at least the first stage of Awakening and become a Sotāpanna. Then it will be impossible to do any action that results in rebirth in the lower realms. This will not necessarily mean that such a person will miss the opportunity to see the next Buddha. Eventually, as a Non-Returner, he or she can be reborn in the Suddhāvāsā Brahma-worlds, and life in these worlds can span the careers of several Buddhas.[1]

If a person who has enough perfections *(pāramī)* to reach Awakening in this lifetime does not make the necessary effort, it may be possible to become a Sotāpanna in the next life in the Deva worlds. If such a person does not practise the factors leading to Awakening, he or she will miss out entirely during this Buddha's Dispensation and will only be able to attain release during the next Buddha's Dispensation.

Ven. Ledi Sayadaw's instructions concerning the necessary work to be done in this life include what should be done by a person who practises bare insight meditation.[2] One should fulfil the first eleven of the fifteen good actions *(caraṇa-dhammā)*,[3] that is to say, all except the Jhāna states. The first four actions

---

[1] See DB II 39-41. Buddha Gotama recounts how the Brahmās in the Suddhāvāsa worlds told him about the six Buddhas before him.

[2] Sukkha-vipassaka, literally, "one who develops 'dry' insight."

[3] Vism, chap. VII, 30f. For a discussion of these, see MLS II 20-25.

are: (1) being moral,[1] (2) guarding the sense doors, (3) being moderate in eating, and (4) wakefulness.

The next seven qualities are the seven good states *(saddhammā)* that the Buddha compared to the various protections for the citizens of a royal border town:[2]

(1) Faith *(saddhā)* in the Buddha is like a deeply embedded pillar.

(2) Modesty *(hiri)* is like a deep, wide moat and means that the disciple is ashamed of wrong conduct in body, speech, and mind.

(3) Shrinking from doing wrong *(ottappa)* is like a high, wide road surrounding the city and means that the disciple is concerned to avoid wrong conduct in body, speech, and mind.

(4) Being of great learning *(bāhu-sacca)* is like a great armoury of spears and swords. A person who has heard much, who remembers what was heard, and who treasures it means a person who knows the Buddha's Doctrine.

(5) Energy *(viriya)* is like a large army protecting the city, for a person should rouse energy to get rid of unskilled mental states, to acquire skilled mental states, to be steadfast, firm in advance, and persevere with skilled mental states.

(6) Mindfulness *(sati)* is like a wise, intelligent gate keeper who refuses entrance to unknown people and only lets in those who are known. A person should have the highest degree of mindfulness and discrimination.

(7) Wisdom *(paññā)* is like a high, wide rampart covered with plaster. A person should possess wisdom leading to (the cutting off of) rise and fall, with the noble penetration leading to the complete destruction of misery.

---

[1] Ven. Ledi Sayadaw says generosity is included here.

[2] See GS III 71-73. We discuss them in the order found there. The Jhānas are added to the seven there.

All seven of these good states enable a person to abandon wrong actions and cultivate good actions, to abandon what is blameworthy and develop blamelessness. Thus he develops purity.

We need not worry about whether we will be able to attain the goal of Nibbāna in this life or whether we will only be able to do so under Buddha Ariya Metteyya. If we make the best effort we can, such questions will take care of themselves. We must grow as much as possible in morality, concentration, and wisdom, confident that in this way we will be able to come to the end of all suffering.

Truth Will Triumph!

Appendix A
Anāgatavaṃsa
The Chronicle of the Future Buddha*

Praise to That One, the Blessed One, the Noble One, the Fully Self-Awakened One

1 Sāriputta of great wisdom, the leader Upatissa, the firm general of the Doctrine, approached the leader of the world

2-3 and asked the Conqueror about his own doubts with reference to the future Buddha: "What will the wise Buddha immediately after you be like? I wish to hear this in detail. Please tell me, O Seeing One." Hearing the Thera's words, the Blessed One said this:

4 It is not possible for anyone to describe at length Ajita's great accumulated merit which is not small, which is of great fame. I will tell (you about) it in part. Listen, O Sāriputta.

5 In this auspicious world cycle, in the future, in a crore of years, there will be an Awakened One named Metteyya, best of men,

6 of great merit, great wisdom, great knowledge, great fame, great power, great steadfastness; he will be born, one who sees.

7 This Conqueror will be born having great retentiveness, mindfulness, wisdom and learning; (he will be) one who has comprehended, known, and seen all things, who has fully

---

* I wish to thank Mr K.R. Norman for his help in translating the Anāgatavaṃsa. I am responsible, of course, for the final version and any mistakes in it. I hope to prepare an edition with full critical apparatus, but this will only be possible after the unpublished commentary has been examined in detail.

William Pruitt

contacted them, fathomed them, and thoroughly grasped them..

8 At that time, there will be a royal city named Ketumatī, twelve leagues long and seven leagues wide,

9 full of men and women, adorned with palaces, frequented by cultured people, invincible, protected by the Dhamma.

10 There will be a king named Saṅkha, of limitless strength and vehicles, possessing the seven jewels, a Wheel-Turning Monarch of great power,

11 having psychic powers, fame, enjoying all sensual pleasures; and he will righteously preach the doctrine of quiescence that destroys all its opponents.

12 A well-made palace there, like a celestial mansion, will arise through his merit. (It will be) resplendent with many jewels,

13 surrounded by balustrades, well designed, delightful, resplendent, very tall, the best, hard to look at, dazzling the eyes.

14 The jewel palace that came into existence for King Mahā-Panādassa will rise up for him and King Saṅkha will live in it.

15 And then, in that city, there will be various streets here and there, well-built lotus ponds, delightful, with well-made banks,

16 full to the brim with clear, clean, sweet, cool, fragrant water, level with the land, and (with banks) strewn with sand,

17 (ponds) covered with red and blue lotuses, accessible to all people at all times. There will be seven rows of palm trees and walls of seven colours

18 made of jewels encircling all the city. The royal city of Kusavātī at that time will be Ketumatī.

19 At the four gate(s) of the city there will be shining wish-fulfilling trees, (one) blue, (one) yellow, (one) red, and (one) white.

20 There will have come into being celestial clothes and celestial ornaments hanging there, all sorts of wealth and possessions.

21 At that time, in the middle of the city, there will be four halls, facing the four directions, and there will be (another) wish-fulfilling tree produced by his merit.

22 Hanging from those wish-fulfilling trees there will be cotton cloth, sheaths, flaxen cloth of Kodum produced by his merit.

23 Hanging from those wish-fulfilling trees there will be tambourines, tambours, and small drums produced by his merit.

24 Hanging from those wish-fulfilling trees there will be encircling bracelets and necklaces made of jewels produced by his merit.

25 Hanging from those wish-fulfilling trees there will be "high" ornaments, "blooming-face" ornaments, bracelets and girdles produced by his merit.

26 And hanging from those wish-fulfilling trees there will be many other ornaments and decorations of different sorts.

27 Through the action of beings' merits, men will enjoy self-generated rice that has no "dust," no chaff, that is pure, sweet-smelling, with grains ready husked, ripened without cultivation.

28 A sixteenth of (today's) *ambaṇa* (measure) will be 2,270 cartloads.

29 And at that time one grain will produce two *tumbas* —they are called rice grains—produced by the action of beings' merits.

30 The men who live in Ketumatī in the kingdom of Saṅkha will wear armour and bracelets.

31 With all their wishes fulfilled, they will be happy, wearing large earrings. Their bodies will be covered with yellow sandalwood paste. They will wear garments from Kāsi.

32 They will be of great wealth, rich; they will be woken by lutes and drums. They will constantly be exceedingly happy in body and mind.

33 Jambudīpa will be ten thousand leagues, without thorns, clear, even, with green grass.

34 There will be three diseases: desire, hunger, and old age. The women will marry at the age of five hundred.

35 They will always be in unity, congenial, without disputes. The vines, trees, and bushes will be laden with fruit and flowers.

36 There will be a grass four-inches high that will be as soft as cotton. There will be even rains and gentle winds, neither too hot nor too cold.

37 There will always be a salubrious climate. The rivers and ponds will not lack (in water). Here and there in the districts, the pure sand will not be rough. It will be scattered around like pearls the size of peas and beans.

38 It will be delightful like an adorned garden. Here and there, there will be villages and towns very close together and full of people.

39 (The villages and towns) will be like a great forest of reeds and bamboo, full of people, I think, without an open space.

40 Trading cities will be filled with men and women who will be prosperous, rich and tranquil, free from danger and in good health.

41 They will wander about festivals, always joyful, always playing, extremely happy. They will rejoice, happy and pleased.

42 There will be much food and water, much to eat, much meat, drink, and water. Jambudīpa will be delightful, like the Āḷakamandā of the Devas or the broad capital of the Kurus.

43-45 One named Ajita (will be born), Metteyya, the best of two-footed beings, with the thirty-two excellent marks and the minor characteristics, of golden complexion, without stain, very splendid, resplendent, of the highest fame, glorious, of perfect form, of good appearance, of great power, incomparable. He will be born in a brahman family, with great wealth and possessions, and of excellent family, heir to an unsullied pedigree.

46 (Four) palaces made of jewels will have come into being for Ajita: Sirivaḍḍha, Vaḍḍhamāna, Siddhattha, and Candaka.

47 Ajita's female attendants will be women perfect in all their limbs, adorned with (all kinds of) ornaments, small, medium, and large.

48 There will be a complete (retinue of) one hundred thousand women fully adorned. Candamukhī will be his wife. Brahmavaddhana will be his son.

49 He will delight in great happiness, be joyful, and endowed with pleasure. He will enjoy all fame as was Vāsava at Nandana.

50 He will live in a household for eight thousand years. At some time, he will go to a park for pleasure to amuse himself.

51 Seeing the danger in sensual pleasures and being wise in accordance with the nature of Bodhisattas, he will see the four signs which destroy sensual pleasures:

52 an old man, a sick man, a dead man, and a happy wanderer. He will go forth. Having sympathy for all beings,

53 he will become averse to sensual pleasures and indifferent to great happiness. He will go forth seeking the unsurpassed state of peace.

54 After undertaking the practice of exertion for seven days, this Great Being, the Conqueror, will go forth, leaping up (into the air) with his palace.

55-56 Ajita will go forth, honoured by a great group of people, friends and companions, blood relatives, a fourfold army, an assembly of the four castes, and 84,000 princesses.

57 When Metteyya has gone forth, at that time, 84,000 brahmans who are skilled in the Vedas will go forth.

58 At that time, both of the brothers, Isidatta and Purāṇa will go forth (with) 84,000 (other people).
59 The twins, Jātimitta and Vijaya, of unlimited wisdom, will serve that Perfect Buddha from the 84,000.
60 The householder named Suddhika and the lay woman Sudhanā will serve that perfect Buddha from the 84,000.
61 The lay disciple named Saṅgha and the lay woman named Saṅghā will serve that perfect Buddha from the 84,000.
62 The householder named Saddhara and the renowned Sudatta will serve that perfect Buddha from the 84,000.
63 The woman named Yasavatī and the renowned Visākhā, with a retinue of 84,000 men and women,
64 will go forth in renunciation on the admonition of Metteyya. Other citizens and many people from the country, and no few nobles, brahmans, merchants, and workers,
65 inclined to renunciation, a great crowd of all sorts of birth, will then go forth, following the going forth of Metteyya.
66 On the day that Wise One goes forth in renunciation, on that very day of renouncing, he will approach the dais of the tree of awakening.
67 In the place of the unconquered Leaders of Men, on that supreme seat of awakening, seated in a cross-legged position, the One of Great Fame will be awakenend.
68 The Conqueror will go to the excellent garden Nāgavana in full flower, and there he will set in motion the incomparable Wheel of the Doctrine:
69 misery, the arising of misery, the overcoming of misery, and the Noble Eightfold Path leading to the cessation of misery.
70 Then, there will be a gathering of men all around for one hundred leagues when that protector of the world sets in motion the Wheel of the Doctrine.
71 Then, very many Devas will approach the Conqueror there, and he will free 1,000 crores from their bondage.

72-73 Then, that king Saṅkha, having given his jewel palace to the Saṅgha with the Conqueror at its head, having given another great gift to beggars and wayfarers, and hurrying along with his queen towards the Perfect Buddha,

74 he of limitless strength and vehicles will come to the Conqueror in great regal splendour, accompanied by 90,000 crores (of people).

75 Then the Perfect Buddha will beat the drum of the Doctrine, the excellent and highest sound of the drum of deathlessness by declaring the Four (Noble) Truths.

76 The company of people accompanying the king, all 90,000 crores without exception, will become "Come Bhikkhu" monks.

77 Then Devas and men will approach the Leader of the World and ask the Conqueror a question concerning Arahatship.

78 That Conqueror will answer them and 80,000 crores will attain Arahatship. That will be the third penetration.

79 The first assembly will be of 100,000 crores of those whose taints are destroyed, who are spotless, of peaceful minds, venerable ones.

80 When the Blessed One proclaims the Invitation (to declare purity) at the end of the rainy season, that Conqueror will be surrounded by 90,000 crores.

81 And when the Sage has gone in seclusion to the golden and silver Gandhamādana slope of the Himavanta mountain range,

82-83 he will enjoy the sport of meditation (accompanied by) 80,000 crores of those whose taints are destroyed, who are spotless, of peaceful minds, venerable ones. 100,000 crores of those who possess the six higher knowledges, who possess great psychic power, will constantly surround that Protector of the World, Metteyya.

84 Those who are skilled in discriminating knowledge, who are proficient in etymology and terminology, who are very

learned, experts in the Doctrine, discerning, adornments of the Saṅgha,

85 well tamed, gentle, firm, will surround that Conqueror. Honoured by those monks, that Nāga (the Buddha) (will travel about) together with those who are Nāgas like him—he who will have crossed over, together with those who have crossed over; he who will have attained peace with those who are peaceful.

86 Accompanied by (his) orders of disciples the Great Sage—the Compassionate One, the Sympathetic One, Metteyya, the greatest of two-footed beings,

87 the Conqueror—will wander through the towns and villages and capitals, raising up many beings, including the Devas, bringing them to Nibbāna.

88 He will beat the drum of the Doctrine. He will sound the conch shell of the Doctrine. He will proclaim the spiritual sacrifice. He will raise the banner of the Doctrine.

89 He will roar the lion's roar, set in motion the excellent wheel (of the Doctrine), and cause men and women to drink the drink of truth with its excellent taste.

90 That Conqueror will wander for the sake of all beings, both rich and poor, causing many people who are capable of being awakened to be awakened.

91 The Seeing One will cause some to take refuge (in the Triple Gem), some to take the five moral precepts, and some to undertake the ten skilful (actions).

92 He will give some the state of recluseship and the four excellent Fruition States. He will give some discriminating knowledge into the incomparable Doctrine.

93 The Seeing One will give some the eight excellent attainments. He will give some the three knowledges and the six higher knowledges.

94 That Conqueror will admonish (a large) group of people (to undertake) that practice. Then the Teaching of the Conqueror Metteyya will be widespread.

95 Seeing people capable of being awakened, that Sage will go 100,000 leagues in a moment and will cause them to be awakened.

96 At that time, Metteyya's mother will be named Brahmavatī, his father will be named Subrahma and will be the head priest of King Saṅkha.

97 His two chief disciples will be Asoka and Brahmadeva. The (lay) attendant Sīha will attend on that Conqueror.

98 Padumā and Sumanā will be his foremost female disciples. Sumana and Saṅgha will be his foremost personal supporters.

99 Yasavatī and Saṅghā will be his foremost female supporters. The Nāga tree will be the awakening (place) for that Blessed One.

100 Its trunk will be two thousand cubits. It will have 20,000 branches with curved tips (always) moving. It will shine like the outspread tail of a peacock.

101 The tips (of the branches) will be continually in flower and fragrant with a heavenly smell. The blossoms will be the size of wheels, with enough pollen to fill a *nāḷi* measure.

102 (The tree) will send its flowers in all directions for ten leagues, both with and against the wind. It will scatter its flowers all around the throne of awakening.

103 People from the country, coming together there, will smell the excellent odour and pour forth words (of admiration), rejoicing in its odour.

104 There will be a happy fruition of meritorious deeds for that venerable one, the Best of Buddhas, whose unimaginable radiance will spread out (like the smell of) the flowers.

105 That Conqueror will be eighty-eight cubits tall. That Teacher's chest will be twenty-five cubits in diameter.

106 The Seer will have broad eyes with thick eyelashes. His eyes will be pure, not blinking day or night. His physical eye will see small or large things

107 in all directions for ten leagues without obstruction. His radiance will stream forth as far as twenty-five leagues.

108 That Conqueror will shine like a streak of lightning or a candlestick. He will shine like the sun, resembling a garland of jewels.

109 His (thirty-two major) marks and (eighty) secondary marks will at all times be seen as rays. Many hundreds of thousands of different sorts of rays will fall down.

110 At every footstep (he takes) a beautiful flowering lotus will grow. (The lotuses will be) thirty cubits (across) with even petals and twenty-five minor petals.

111 The stamens will be twenty cubits long and the pericaps will be sixteen cubits long. Inside the red lotuses (the flowers) will be filled with very red pollen.

112 The Devas of the sense-sphere heavens will make columns of honour and Nāga kings and Supaṇṇa (Devas) will decorate them.

113 There will be eight columns of gold, eight of silver, eight of jewels, and eight made of coral.

114 There will be many hundreds of flags hanging there disporting themselves—adorned garlands of flags ornamented with many precious gems.

115 There will be awnings adorned with jewels, pearls and garlands, resembling the moon. There will be many jewelled head ornaments with nets of small bells surrounding them.

116 They will scatter fragrant, sweet-smelling, perfumed flowers, and different sorts of powder, both human and celestial,

117 and a variety of cloths of diverse colours, beautiful, of the five colours. They will all sport around, having faith in the Buddha.

118 There will be gateways there with strings of jewels, a thousand (cubits) high, delightful, beautiful, unobstructed and well-formed.
119 They will be seen to be shining, with their radiance widespread all around. The Buddha, at the head of the Order of Monks, will go in their midst,
120 like Brahmā in his assembly or lnda in his palace. When the Buddha goes (anywhere), they will go; when he stays (in a place), they will stay;
121 when the Teacher sits or lies down together with his assembly, they will always practise the (same) four postures.
122 There will be these honours as well as others, both human and celestial. There will constantly be many sorts of marvels
123 to honour Metteyya through the power of his endless merit. Having seen that marvel, many people of various births, (many) men with their families, will only abandon the Teacher as their refuge at the cost of their lives.
124 Those who practise the holy life after hearing the word of the Sage will go beyond the cycle of existence, which is subject to death and difficult to escape from.
125 Many householders will purify the eye of the Doctrine by means of the ten meritorious acts and the three types of right action.
126 Many will be destined for heaven through being accomplished in the traditional learning and texts, having purified (themselves) through respect for him, and through following the true Doctrine.
127 It would not be possible to describe in every detail their fame which will be so great. They will be continually very happy. When they reach the end of their time (in that life),
128 those men will have great fame as well as happiness. Life, beauty, and strength, and heavenly bliss (in a heavenly world) will be theirs.

129 They will experience the happiness of sensual pleasures for as long as they wish. Then afterwards, at the end of their lives, they will enter into (true) happiness.

130 (The Buddha's) lifetime there will be 80,000 years. Remaining there that long, he will bring many people to the other shore.

131 He will cause beings whose minds are ripe to be completely awakened and he will instruct others who have not perceived the (four) truths as to which is the right path and which is the wrong path.

132 He will carefully establish the torch of the Doctrine, the boat of the Doctrine, the mirror of the Doctrine, and the medicine (of the Doctrine) for beings (at that time and) in the future.

133 Then, in the midst of the venerable order of disciples who will have done what should be done, that Conqueror will blaze out like a mass of fire, and be extinguished.

134 When the Perfect Buddha has been completely extinguished, his Teaching will remain for 180,000 years. After that, there will be a terrible disappearance of the true Doctrine in the world.

135 Thus, the constituent elements are impermanent, not firm, temporary, and states of being are transitory, liable to destruction and old age, and empty.

136 The constituent elements are like an empty fist, they are empty, they are the talk of fools. There is no power for anyone there, not even for one who has the psychic powers.

137 Thus, knowing this as it really is, one should be disillusioned with all compounded things. A Thoroughbred Among Men is hard to find. He is not born everywhere. Wherever that Hero is born, that happy family prospers.

138 Therefore, in order to see Buddha Metteyya here, act rightly, firmly, energetically, with agitated mind.

139 Whoever does good things here and dwells vigilent, whether a monk, nun, lay disciple, or laywoman disciple,
140 whoever esteems the great Buddha, pays great honour to the Great One, that person together with the Devas will see the auspicious assembly at that time.
141 Practise the holy life. Give suitable gifts. Keep the observance days. Practise loving kindness carefully.
142 Be one who delights in being vigilent, always performing meritorious actions. Having acted skilfully here, you will make an end of misery.

Appendix B:

Aspirations to Meet Buddha Ariya Metteyya

We have made some alterations in the following translations.[1]

1. Aspiration concluding many Pāḷi manuscripts in Sri Lanka (from Dbk, p. 36):

> By the merit of this writing may I draw near to Metteyya (and) having been established in the Refuges, may I be well established in the Sāsana.

2. Aspiration concluding manuscripts in Sinhalese (from Dbk, p. 37):

> By the power of these meritorious deeds, without falling into the four hells, may I seek the Bodhisatta Metteyya in the Tāvatiṃsa heaven and enjoying divine happiness, and going from there to Ketumatī City, eradicating the defilements, may I receive the peace of liberation from the Buddha Metteyya.

3. Aspiration concluding the Dvādasaparitta (from Dbk, p. 38):

> In the future, Buddha Metteyya will be unexcelled in the world, he of great merits, of great power; may you have great peace.

---

[1]See *Culte*, pp. 559-560, for the formula recited by lay people in Sri Lanka and the exhortation of the bhikkhus to the lay people to aspire to rebirth in the Deva worlds in their next life in order to eventually encounter Metteyya, hear him preach, and attain liberation.

4. Aspiration attributed to King Parākramabāhu I of Sri Lanka (from Dbk, p. 38):

> Having departed from here and being reborn on the peak of Himalaya in the noble Jambudīpa (India) as a leading deity of an aeon's life-span, I shall indeed hear the Doctrine of Lord Metteyya.

5. Aspiration at the conclusion of the commentary on the Jātaka (from Dbk, p. 39; verses 4-11 of the concluding 37 verses):

> May I, through this meritorious deed, be born in my next life in the city of Tusita, the beautiful dwelling-place of the gods. May I listen to the preaching of Lord Metteyya and enjoy great glory with him for a long time. When this Great Being is born in the charming city of Ketumatī as the Buddha, may I be reborn with the three noble root-conditions in a brahman family. May I make offerings to that Great Sage of invaluable robes of the finest sort, alms, dwelling-places and medicines in abundance. May I undertake the life of a bhikkhu in the dispensation and illumine that noble (institution), being the possessor of potency, mindful and well-versed in the Tipiṭaka. May he predict (of me), "This one will be a Buddha in the future." And may I offer gifts to the Buddhas who will come one after the other and (receive sure prediction) from them too. May I fare on in repeated births, give food and other things that are desired like a wish-conferring tree. May I fulfil all the perfections of morality, renunciation, wisdom, and so forth, and having attained the summit of the perfections, become an incomparable Buddha. May I preach the sweet Doctrine which brings bliss to all beings, liberating the whole world with its Devas from the bondage of repeated births. May I guide them to the most excellent, tranquil Nibbāna.

6. Aspiration at the conclusion of Sinhalese manuscripts of Ācariya Buddhaghosa's Visuddhimagga (*The Path of Purification,* pp. 837f.):

By the performance of such merit
As has been gained by me through this
And any other still in hand
So may I in my next becoming
Behold the joys of Tāvatiṃsa,
Glad in the qualities of virtue
And unattached to sense desires
By having reached the first fruition,
And having in my last life seen
Metteyya, Lord of Sages, highest
Of persons in the world, and helper
Delighting in all beings' welfare,
And heard the Holy One proclaim
The teaching of the Noble Law,
May I grace the Victor's Dispensation
By realizing its Highest Fruit.

7. The aspiration of Thera Mahā-Maṅgala in his biography of Ācariya Buddhaghosa (Buddhaghosuppatti) (from Dbk, p. 40):

O may it be my lot to meet with him, the Lord Metteyya! He, the Fully Awakened One, shall lead vast multitudes across *saṃsāra's* stream.

When I have found Metteyya, may I be versed in the three scriptures, and then in wisdom I shall see face-to-face the lord of mercy.

8. Aspiration at the end of sharing merits in the Dāna ceremony in Sri Lanka (from Dbk, p. 41):

By the aid of this meritorious deed of Dāna, may you be reborn in the heavenly and human worlds, enjoying the greatest of worldly happiness, and may you be born again in the presence of Buddha Metteyya, and benefiting from his teaching of the Four Noble Truths, may you attain to the supreme, immortal, great Nibbāna!

9. Aspiration used in connection with the recitation of Parittas (verses of protection) in Sri Lanka (from Dbk, p. 42):

> May the multitude of gods dwelling over the seven oceans, on Mount Meru, in the Titans' world, in the world of Nāgas, in the six celestial worlds, in the four shrines of the (four Guardian) Devas, on Mount Samantakūṭa, on the Himalayas, over the seven lakes, over Lake Anotatta, in the sky, on the earth, in all the Brahma-worlds, in this Cakkavāḷa (world-system), in the island of Ceylon, partake of these merits with loving thoughts and perceive Nibbāna by seeing the sage-king Metteyya.

10. Closing verses at the end of Sinhalese manuscripts of Ācariya Buddhaghosa's Atthasālinī (U Pe Maung Tin's translation, *The Expositor*, p. 542):

> By grace of this, the book I wrote,
> Into Metteyya's presence am I come.
> Within the Refuges established
> Upon the Sāsana I take my stand.
> May mother, father, teachers, they who wish me well
> And they who do not, give me happy thanks
> And long safeguard the merit I have won.

Worldwide Contact Address in the Tradition of Sayagyi U Ba Khin

International Meditation Centre
31A Inya Myaing Road
Bahan Post Office
Yangon, Myanmar

International Meditation Centre
Splatts Houset
Heddington, Calne
Wiltshire SN11 OPE, U.K.
Tel.: +44 380 850 238
Fax: +44 380 850 833

International Meditation Centre
Lot 78, Jacoby Street
Mahogany Creek, WA 60724
Australia
Tel.: +61 9 295 2544
Fax: +61 9 295 3435

International Meditation Centre
Lot 2, Cessnock Road
Sunshine, NSW 2264
Australia
Tel.: +61 49 705 433
Fax: +61 49 705 749

International Meditation Centre
446 Bankard Road
Westminster MD 21158, U.S.A.
Tel.: +1 410 346 7889
Fax: +1 410 346 7282

International Meditation Centre
A-9064 St. Michael/Gurk 6
Austria
Tel.: +43 4224 2820
Fax: +43 4224 2820

Sayagyi U Ba Khin Gesellschaft
Greyerzstrasse 35
3013 Bern, Switzerland
Tel.: +41 31 415 233

Sayagyi U Ba Khin Stichting
Oudegracht 12
3511 AW Utrecht
The Netherlands
Tel.: +31 30 311 445
Fax: +31 30 340 612

Sayagyi U Ba Khin Gesellschaft
Näherweg 41
7520 Bruchsal, Germany
Tel.: +49 7251 89148
Fax: +49 7251 89148

Sayagyi U Ba Khin Memorial Association, Singapore
24-04A 23rd Floor
International Plaza
10F Anson Road
Singapore
Tel.: +65 22 05 031
+65 44 96 110